FINANCE THEORY AND ASSET PRICING

FINANCE THEORY AND ASSET PRICING

Frank Milne

CLARENDON PRESS · OXFORD
1995

Oxford University Press, Walton Street, Oxford OX2 6DP
Oxford New York
Athens Auckland Bangkok Bombay
Calcutta Cape Town Dar es Salaam Delhi
Florence Hong Kong Istanbul Karachi
Kuala Lumpur Madras Madrid Melbourne
Mexico City Nairobi Paris Singapore
Taipei Tokyo Toronto
and associated companies in
Berlin Ibadan

Oxford is a trade mark of Oxford University Press

Published in the United States
by Oxford University Press Inc., New York

British Library Cataloguing in Publication Data
Data available

Library of Congress Cataloging in Publication Data
Milne, Frank.
Finance theory and asset pricing / Frank Milne.
p. cm.
Includes bibliographical references and index.
1. Finance—Mathematical models. 2. Capital assets pricing model.
I. Title.
HG174.M554 1995 94–36056 332—dc20

ISBN 0–19–877397–8
ISBN 0–19–877398–6 (Pbk.)

1 3 5 7 9 10 8 6 4 2

Typeset by Pure Tech Corporation, Pondicherry, India
Printed in Great Britain
on acid-free paper by
Bookcraft (Bath) Ltd., Midsomer Norton, Avon

Contents

Introduction

This book is based on a set of lectures that I gave at the Institute of Advanced Studies in Vienna in 1992, and subsequently taught in the Economics Department, Queen's University. My brief was to provide a series of ten lectures that surveyed and introduced recent asset-pricing models in Finance, using mathematical techniques and microeconomic theory at the level of Varian's *Microeconomic Analysis*, or Kreps's *A Course in Microeconomic Theory*. With these prerequisites the book should be accessible to any first-year graduate student who has a good grounding in microeconomics. Necessarily this book is not complete, and omits much that is important in terms of generality and detail. To make the book complete in that sense would triple its length and increase the level of mathematical difficulty substantially.

The first chapter provides a brief history of modern finance theory, emphasizing the main contributions and sketching the role of application in the development of the theory. Chapter 2 introduces the two-date model with complete markets and uncertainty. The chapter recalls standard microeconomic arguments and introduces some of the geometric arguments that are developed more fully later in the book. Chapter 3 generalizes the model by allowing for incomplete markets and non-trivial asset markets. In Chapter 4 the incomplete market economy equilibrium is analysed using the idea of induced preferences and production sets over assets. This idea allows us to construct geometric proofs of arbitrage results and relate them to familiar microeconomic theoretical arguments. The Modigliani–Miller arguments on capital structure and the binomial option-pricing model are introduced as illustrations of the general argument. Chapter 5 covers the same ground but uses the technique of personalized martingale pricing as an alternative method for analysing the same problems. Chapter 6 considers asset-pricing models with consumer aggregation when arbitrage arguments are not possible. The arguments are geometric and avoid functional forms except as illustrations from the literature. Chapter 7 discusses diversification arguments using induced preferences, and establishes the equilibrium arbitrage-pricing theory when there is a finite number of assets. The capital asset-pricing model is deduced as a special case of the general theorem. Chapter 8 extends the two-date model to a multi-date complete market structure, and introduces some preliminary results. Chapter 9 explores arbitrage pricing in the complete market model and illustrates the ideas with the multiperiod binomial option-pricing model. The last chapter allows for incomplete markets and shows how previous results can be extended into a multi-period incomplete-markets framework. The book ends with a brief conclusion discussing extensions of the models and recent developments in asset-pricing models.

I wish to thank my students and colleagues at Queen's for many comments on earlier drafts of this book. Also I would like to thank the Institute of Advanced Studies for suggesting this project; and the Canadian SSHRCC for funding. I would like to thank Linda Freeman for her help in preparing and typing this manuscript in WordPerfect, and those at OUP involved in its publication.

1

A Brief History of Finance Theory

The history of finance theory is an interesting example of the interaction between abstract theorizing and practical application. Many of the original contributions in finance theory began as theoretical abstractions that appeared to be of limited or no practical use. But with additional assumptions and restrictions, these same theories have become commonplace in the major financial markets as standard frames of reference in analysing financial decisions and the functioning of markets. In addition, what had once been seen as a group of related theories can now be unified within a general framework. These developments have taken place in a relatively short space of time: the original ideas were developed in the 1950s, and culminated in the general theoretical structures published in the 1980s.

THE IMPORTANT CONTRIBUTIONS OF THE 1950s

To understand the current state of finance theory, we should go back to the fundamental contributions of Arrow (1963)—first published in French in 1953—and Debreu (1959). Their contribution was fundamental in showing how the economic model under certainty could be adapted to incorporate uncertainty. The basic idea was very simple: the commodity space was expanded to incorporate possible future states of the world. The market system was complete in the sense that there was a set of contingent markets for all commodities. Standard theorems on the existence and Pareto optimality of competitive equilibria could be reinterpreted, so that one could have an efficient allocation of resources under uncertainty. Although not recognized at the time, this abstract economy was the foundation for much of what was to follow.

Two other important theoretical developments occurred in the 1950s. In 1958, Modigliani and Miller published a controversial paper arguing that the financial structure of firms was a matter of indifference for all agents in the economy. Their proof relied upon the idea that individuals could employ a riskless arbitrage to undo the variation in the firm's financial structure. Although originally couched in terms of the firm's choice over debt and equity, it became apparent that the argument was general and could be applied to changes in dividend policy, debt structure, or other financial decisions. (See Miller, 1988 for a detailed account of these ideas.) The major novelty in the Modigliani–Miller paper was the use of financial arbitrage. In the coming decades, arbitrage arguments were to play an important role in understanding a whole array of complex asset-pricing problems.

The other major development was the publication of Markowitz's (1959) monograph on mean-variance portfolio selection. The basic idea was quite straightforward: if consumers were concerned about the average, and variability of portfolio returns, then one could obtain a simple analysis of portfolio choice in terms of the means and covariances of the original assets. This contribution was the first step in the development of portfolio analysis and asset pricing based on mean-variance analysis.

THE 1960s: THEORY AND THE BEGINNINGS OF APPLICATION

There were two major developments in finance theory in the 1960s. The first extended the Arrow–Debreu theory to explore financial markets in more detail. Hirshleifer (1965, 1966) made an important contribution by showing how the Arrow–Debreu theory could be applied to basic finance problems. In particular, he proved the Modigliani–Miller financial irrelevance result in the Arrow–Debreu framework. This was the first time that Arrow–Debreu had been linked to arbitrage theory.

These papers were followed quickly by Diamond's (1967) paper investigating the implications of incomplete asset markets. Diamond showed, in a two-date model under uncertainty, that with exogenously specified asset markets, the competitive equilibrium is a constrained optimum. Furthermore, he showed that one could obtain the Modigliani–Miller theorem so long as the bonds did not have default risk.

The second major development in the 1960s was the extension of the Markowitz mean-variance analysis to a competitive economy. Sharpe (1964), Lintner (1965), and Mossin (1966) observed that, with market clearance, all consumers would choose portfolios that were a linear combination of the risk-free asset and the market portfolio. A direct consequence of that observation is that equilibrium asset prices can be written as a linear combination of the bond price and the market value of the market portfolio. Or, in more familiar terms, the expected rate of return on any asset can be written as the risk-free rate of interest plus the asset's normalized covariance with the market times the difference between market's expected rate of return and the risk-free rate. This model and the pricing result became known as the capital asset-pricing model (CAPM). For the first time finance theory had created a simple model relating asset returns that could (in principle) be tested with econometric methods. By the late 1960s these tests were being carried out at the University of Chicago using the newly acquired CRSP share price data. The full flowering of this empirical research was to come in the next decade.

THE 1970s: THEORETICAL AND EMPIRICAL FINANCE COME OF AGE

There were a number of major developments in finance theory in the 1970s. The first was a continuation of the CAPM research programme, extending the model to a multiperiod economy (Merton, 1973*a*), introducing restrictions on borrowing (Black, 1972), introducing transaction costs (Milne and Smith, 1980), and applying it to a range of empirical problems in finance. As an empirical model CAPM began to have a major impact on the way investors and mutual fund managers controlled portfolios and assessed their performance. (For an informal discussion of the impact of these ideas see Bernstein, 1992.)

The second major contribution grew out of dissatisfaction with empirical tests of the CAPM. Although initial testing of CAPM appeared to show that the theory provided good fits to the data, subsequent work (Roll, 1977) showed that the predictive power of CAPM was exaggerated by the test methodology. Ross (1976) introduced the arbitrage-pricing theory (APT) as a generalized competitor to CAPM. By amalgamating pure arbitrage and diversification arguments he showed that one could obtain asset prices as a linear function of a few basic factors. Potentially, the model appeared more flexible and robust than CAPM, and possibly immune to the testing problems associated with CAPM. As we shall see, the APT played a more important role in asset-pricing theory in the following decade.

The third advance in finance theory has had a dramatic impact on theory, and practical financial decisions in capital markets. Black and Scholes (1972) and Merton (1973*b*) showed that one could exploit an arbitrage argument to obtain a relatively simple formula for a call stock option. This result led to the rapid development of a whole range of variations on this model. (See Smith, 1976 for a survey of the advances of that period.) Finance traders and bankers were interested in the models for providing pricing formulae for an ever-increasing array of derivative financial assets being traded in financial markets. Because these models exploited techniques used in physics (i.e. stock returns follow a diffusion process, Ito's lemma is used to obtain the arbitrage hedge, and the solution to a heat exchange equation is employed to derive the formula) there arose a mystique about derivative asset-pricing associated with a popular 'rocket scientist' image. In an important contribution Cox, Ross, and Rubinstein (1979) showed that the Black–Scholes logic and pricing derivation could be greatly simplified. Assuming an elementary binomial stochastic process for the stock it is easy to use arbitrage arguments to derive a binomial option-pricing formula. In addition they showed that by taking appropriate limits, one could obtain the Black–Scholes formula. Although not stressed in the paper, the underlying model used arbitrage arguments to derive Arrow–Debreu prices, so that the pricing formula was a discounted martingale with Arrow–Debreu prices acting as probabilities.

Another interesting development was the derivation by Rubinstein (1976) of the Black–Scholes formula from a discrete-time incomplete markets equilibrium model. By assuming consumer aggregation, the economy achieved a trivial Pareto optimal allocation and the Arrow–Debreu prices supported the consumer optimum. This was the first representative consumer model where the martingale pricing result was obtained, albeit in a restricted form. In the next decade this general insight was exploited in finance, and particularly in macroeconomic representative consumer models following Lucas (1978).

The idea of martingale pricing was exploited in detail by Harrison and Kreps (1979). They showed that the martingale binomial logic could be generalized to a more abstract setting with continuous or discrete asset-price processes.

This abstract approach was to have a big impact on finance theory in the following decade in sorting out ambiguity that had arisen over the efficient-markets hypothesis (EMH). The idea of the EMH was first introduced by Fama (1970). Building on the earlier work of Samuelson (1965) and earlier writers, he argued that, in financial markets with free entry, no agent could make abnormal returns by exploiting publicly available information. This simple idea was to have a profound impact on empirical finance and the way agents in financial markets viewed their role and performance (see Bernstein, 1992). One of the early problems with the theory was its lack of coherence in making a link with asset-pricing models. This ambiguity was clarified in the 1980s using the theoretical ideas of martingale pricing.

There were two further significant developments. The first was the elaboration and analysis of complete and incomplete asset markets with multiple commodities and finite and infinite time-horizons. The work of Radner (1972) and Hart (1974, 1975) was important in clarifying the properties of incomplete markets. Unfortunately this work and related work on transaction costs in asset trading, introducing money into the model, the objective function of the firm with incomplete markets, and other generalizations, were largely ignored by finance theorists for nearly two decades.

The other major innovation was the introduction of recently developed ideas in asymmetric information into finance theory. Grossman (1976) analysed stock markets where agents had asymmetric information, and explored the idea that stock prices could completely or partially reveal private information. These ideas were explored in detail by a number of writers. (See Huang and Litzenberger, 1988 for a brief review.)

Asymmetric information ideas were introduced to explore the theory of corporate finance when there were differences in information between shareholders and management. These theories examined the robustness of the Modigliani–Miller theorem, when financial structure could act as a signal, or as an incentive mechanism. (See Huang and Litzenberger, 1988; or Bhattacharya and Constantinides, 1989: ii for a review of this literature.)

Because this book concentrates on competitive symmetric information models we will not discuss this large and interesting research topic of asymmetric information and game-theoretic models in finance.

THE 1980s AND BEYOND: THEORETICAL CONSOLIDATION AND UNIFICATION

In the 1980s the advances in theory were largely unifying and extending the existing theories. The various ideas were unified under the general Arrow–Debreu framework, and shown to be very flexible in application. This flexibility proved to be important in understanding the rapidly expanding market in derivative securities. In particular, the hedging and pricing of a whole array of securities became a major industry. Perhaps the most spectacular example of a derivative security was the development of portfolio insurance. This was an application of option-hedging ideas to portfolio management. Although simple in principle, the idea was developed into a significant financial product by two Berkeley finance theorists—Hayne Leland and Mark Rubinstein (see Bernstein, 1992).

On the theoretical front, the martingale idea became a central tool in characterizing asset-pricing in arbitrage or

Arrow–Debreu economies. Using the general idea of stochastic integrals, the models of Black–Scholes and Merton were generalized significantly by Harrison and Pliska (1981), Duffie and Huang (1985), and Duffie (1986).

A more specialized version of those models was introduced by Cox, Ingersoll, and Ross (1985*a*, 1985*b*) to explore the implications of stochastic interest rates for asset-pricing. This model stimulated a series of papers extending the hedging idea to derivative securities defined over bonds, or associated with bonds—see Heath, Jarrow, and Morton (1992) or Jarrow (1992).

Recalling the Rubinstein (1976) equilibrium approach to the Black–Scholes pricing formula, Turnbull and Milne (1991) were able to construct an equilibrium (possibly incomplete market) model that paralleled the Heath, Jarrow, and Morton results and applications. This provided a striking illustration of a more general idea that martingale asset-pricing could be obtained via equilibrium or arbitrage arguments (see Milne and Turnbull, 1994). For practical asset-pricing it is important to construct an argument (either arbitrage or equilibrium) that reduces the general martingale measure to a simpler density that can be written as a function of a small number of observable variables, simulated numerically on a lattice (for a survey see Jarrow, 1992), or approximated by polynomial methods (Madan and Milne, 1992).

Another advance was the clarification of Ross's APT. Two alternative approaches were taken: the first exploited an approximation argument (Chamberlain, 1983; Chamberlain and Rothschild, 1983; Huberman, 1983); the second used general equilibrium arguments to provide an exact or approximate APT (Connor, 1984; Milne 1988).

The APT idea of pricing factors has permeated asset-pricing models, so that many models can be seen as static or dynamic factor-pricing theories. In particular, dynamic asset-pricing models based on diffusion processes can be viewed as a special case of a more general dynamic factor model. Furthermore, by taking an appropriate basis, simple discrete models can mimic their more complex continuous-time counterparts. This discrete model provides an accessible and highly flexible framework for integrating asset-pricing theory (see Milne and Turnbull, 1994 for a detailed discussion of this model and its applications.) In addition the model can be adapted to incorporate fiat money and nominal asset returns, multiple currencies and exchange rates, transaction costs, taxes, and many other features. These variations have been developed recently, or are in the process of development.

This unification of finance theory has found a parallel in modern macroeconomics, where representative agent economies have been analysed to investigate real and pricing variables. Clearly macroeconomics and finance theory exploit the same underlying Arrow–Debreu model. It is hardly surprising that the same Modigliani–Miller type of results reappear in discussions of government financing and open-market operations (in the guise of Ricardian equivalence theorems). Increasingly this literature and finance have become integrated so that the boundaries of the two disciplines are blurred.

SUMMARY

The development of finance theory has been rapid. Not only has it provided highly flexible models, but they have found wide application in financial markets. These developments have been important in providing a coherent framework for thinking about existing financial markets and decision-making; and for creating ways of thinking about new financial products.

It is ironic that abstract ideas developed in the 1950s and 1960s, which once were thought to have limited application, should become the common language of financial markets.

2

Two-Date Models: Complete Markets

In the early 1950s Arrow and Debreu introduced a simple extension to the existing theory of a competitive equilibrium. Consider two dates: today there is certainty and tomorrow there is uncertainty, with $s = 1, \ldots, S$, states of the world. To make life simple, assume there is only one physical commodity, at each date or state. By expanding the definition of the commodity space to include dates and states, we can use all the standard tools of price theory under certainty to analyse an economy with contingent consumption and production. We begin with the

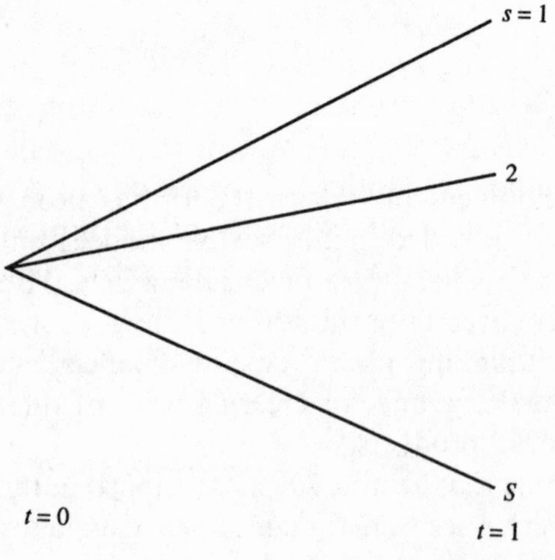

Fig. 2.1

consumer's problem. Each consumer $i = 1, \ldots, I$, has the problem:

$$\underset{\{x_i \in X_i\}}{\text{Max}} \; U_i(x_{0i}, x_{1i}, \ldots, x_{Si})$$

$$s.t \; p_0 x_{0i} + \sum_s p_s x_{si} \equiv W_{0i}$$

where: (i) the utility function is standard neoclassical (i.e. strictly increasing, quasi-concave, differentiable (if necessary));

(ii) p_0 is the price at $t = 0$ of the commodity; p_s is the price at $t = 0$ of the contingent commodity s and

(iii) W_{0i} is the $t = 0$ wealth of the consumer i.

We can analyse the consumer problem using the same tools as the certainty theory. For example, we can derive an indirect utility function, expenditure function, and obtain a Slutsky decomposition of consumer demand. (For details see Varian, 1992.)

Using the same idea we can analyse the firm's problem. Consider firm $f = 1, \ldots, F$, to have the problem:

$$\underset{\{y_j \in Y_j\}}{\text{Max}} \; \sum_{s=1}^{S} p_s y_{sj} - p_0 y_{0j} \equiv \boldsymbol{p}\boldsymbol{y}_j,$$

where $\boldsymbol{p}$ and $\boldsymbol{y}_j$ are the price and production vectors respectively. The firm maximizes its net present value by choosing the most profitable contingent production plan in the production set Y_j, where y_{0j} is the first-date input and y_{sj} the output of contingent commodity s. Again this is identical to the standard theory of the firm, and can be analysed with the same tools (e.g. profit function, cost functions. For details see Varian, 1992).

We can close the system by requiring market-clearing prices for commodity markets.

DEFINITION *A competitive equilibrium for the contingent claims economy is*

a price vector $(p_0^*, p_1^*, \ldots, p_S^*)$;

consumer demands $\boldsymbol{x}_i^* \equiv (x_{0i}^*, x_{1i}^*, \ldots, x_{si}^*)$ $i \in I$;
firm production plans $(\boldsymbol{y}_j^*)$, $j \in J$; *such that*:

(*a*) $\boldsymbol{x}_i^*$ solves: Max $U_i(\boldsymbol{x}_i)$

$$s.t.\ \boldsymbol{p}^* \boldsymbol{x}_i \leqslant \boldsymbol{p}^* \bar{\boldsymbol{x}}_i + \sum_{j \in J} \theta_{ij} \boldsymbol{p}^* \boldsymbol{y}_j^*,$$

where $1 \geqslant \theta_{ij} \geqslant 0$ and $\sum_i \theta_{ij} = 1$, are consumer shares in firm profits;

(*b*) $\boldsymbol{y}_j^*$ solves: $\underset{y_j \in Y_j}{\text{Max}}\ \boldsymbol{p}^* \boldsymbol{y}_j$;

(*c*) $\sum_i \boldsymbol{x}_i^* = \sum_i \bar{\boldsymbol{x}}_i + \sum_j \boldsymbol{y}_j^*$.

There are two important observations one can make about this equilibrium:

1. You can show that under reasonable conditions an equilibrium for this economy exists. (See Varian, 1992 or Debreu, 1959 for more detailed discussions.)
2. You can show by standard techniques the following important results linking a competitive equilibrium with the concept of an efficient, or Pareto optimal allocation.

FIRST FUNDAMENTAL THEOREM OF WELFARE ECONOMICS: *Given a competitive equilibrium with neoclassical consumers, then the equilibrium is a Pareto optimum.*

Comment. Varian (1992) or Debreu (1959) prove this result using weaker assumptions on consumer preferences than our convenient neoclassical assumptions.

SECOND FUNDAMENTAL THEOREM OF WELFARE ECONOMICS: *Given a Pareto optimal allocation*

$$[(\boldsymbol{x}_i^*), (\boldsymbol{y}_j^*)],$$

neoclassical preferences, and convex Y_j, *then there exists prices* $\boldsymbol{p}^*$ *and a general equilibrium which will support that allocation.*

Comment. Varian (1992) or Debreu (1959) prove this result using weaker assumptions on preferences than we assume here.

The two theorems can be illustrated in two commodity examples. Indeed, one can think of the theorems as abstract generalizations of the geometric examples 2.2, 2.3, and 2.4.

1. Pure Exchange: Single Consumer

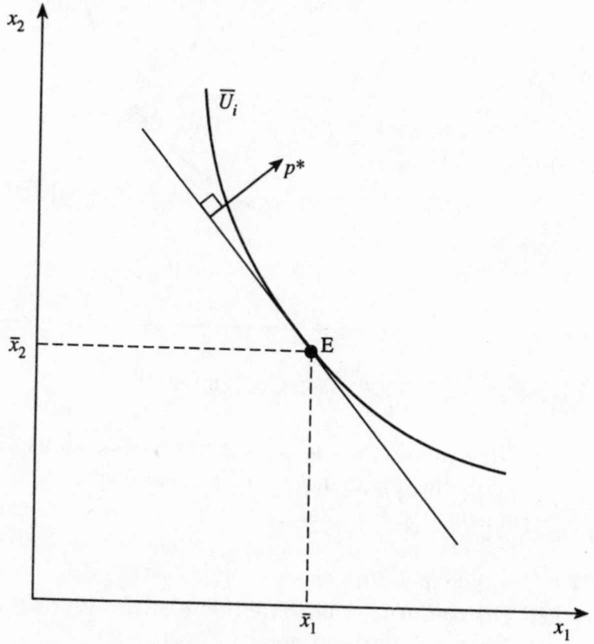

Fig. 2.2 Pure Exchange: Single Consumer

Notes: (1) The supporting prices depend upon the endowment *and* the utility function. Change either and you change the prices.
(2) The allocation E is Pareto optimal trivially.
(3) We can think of the two commodities as commodities at $t=0$ and $t=1$ (with certainty); or as two contingent

commodities at $s = 1, 2$, ignoring consumption at the first date.

2. Pure Exchange: Two Consumers

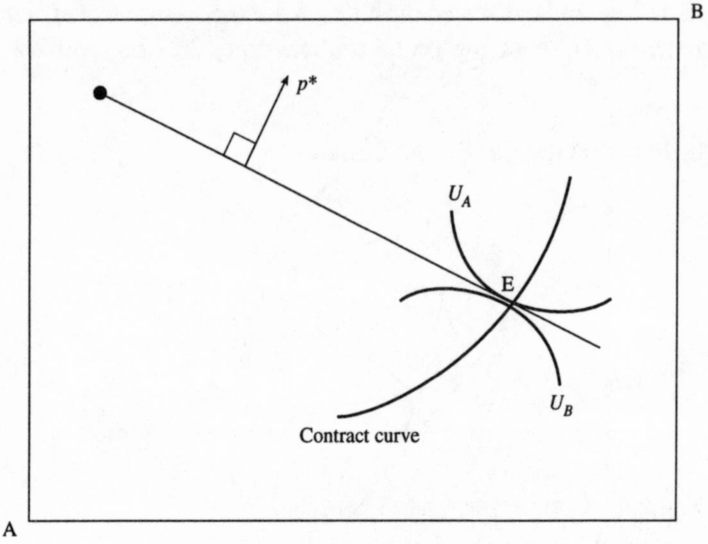

Fig. 2.3 Pure Exchange: Two Consumers

Notes: (1) Now the prices *and* consumption allocations depend upon the preferences *and* the endowments, of both consumers. By altering the division of the aggregate endowment, the competitive allocation and prices will change (in general).

(2) The competitive allocation E is on the contract curve, i.e. it is Pareto optimal.

3. Consumption and Production

Notes: (1) Assume that the $t = 0$ commodity is not consumed, and all of the endowment is used as an input to produce contingent production (y_1, y_2). This contingent production is consumed (x_1, x_2).

(2) The competitive allocation E is Pareto optimal trivially.

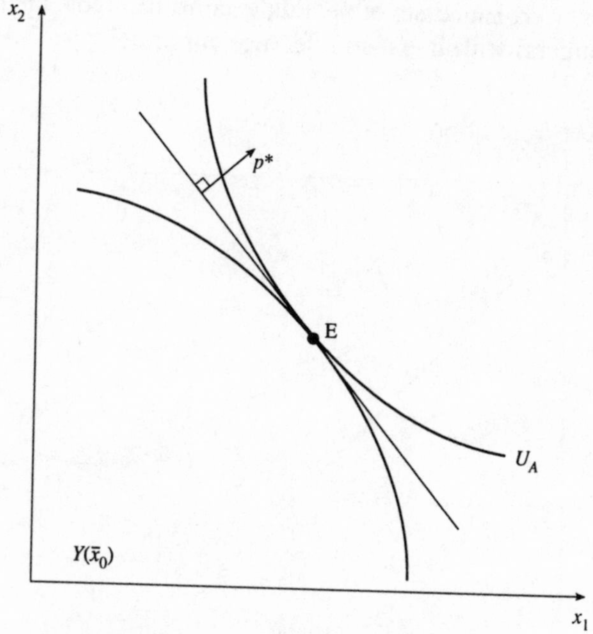

Fig. 2.4 Consumption and Production

CHARACTERIZING PRICES

Unlike much of the standard microeconomic theory, which emphasizes comparative static results, finance theory emphasizes conditions on preferences, production technology, and endowments that restrict relative prices so that we can predict asset prices with some formula. There are two basic tricks that are used.

1. Arbitrage between Perfect Substitute Assets

The idea is very simple: two commodities or assets that are viewed as perfect substitutes will, in equilibrium, sell for the same price.

Consider the case of a single consumer (or identical consumers) with linear indifference curves (Figure 2.5).

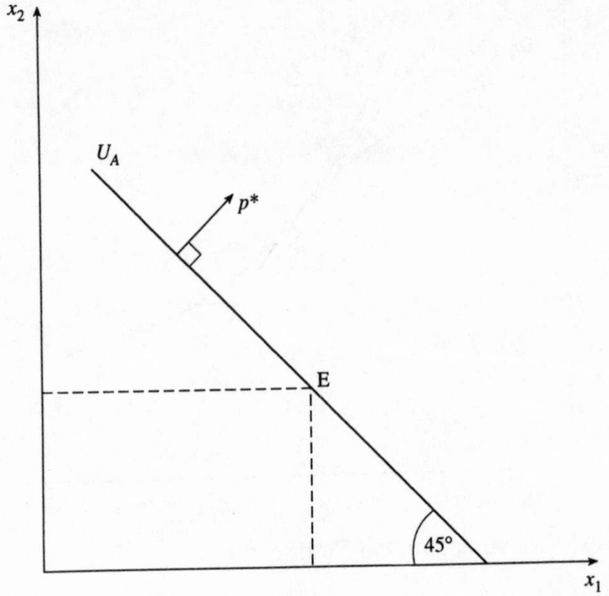

Fig. 2.5

Notes: (1) Given the consumer views (x_1, x_2) as perfect substitutes then equilibrium prices have the property $p_1^* = p_2^*$. Thus if we know p_1^*, automatically we can 'price' p_2^*.

(2) Although the example looks trivial, we will see many sophisticated applications of this principle throughout this book.

2. Consumer Aggregation

This technique is used when arbitrage arguments are not applicable. The fundamental idea is very simple: assume that either all consumers are identical (a representative consumer); or assume that they differ in a restricted sense that wealth redistributions will not alter relative prices. For more details of this approach see Varian (1992, sect. 9.4).

THEOREM: *If each consumer in the economy has a neoclassical utility function which is quasi-homothetic, i.e.*

$$U_i(\boldsymbol{x}_i) \equiv u_i(\alpha_i + \beta \boldsymbol{x}_i)$$

where $u_i() = u()$ is homothetic, then there exists a representative consumer with preferences

$$U_R(\boldsymbol{x}_R) \equiv u\left(\sum_i \alpha_i + \beta \boldsymbol{x}_R\right)$$

and a budget constraint which is the sum of the individual budget constraints.

Consider the case of two consumers in an exchange economy (Figure 2.6).

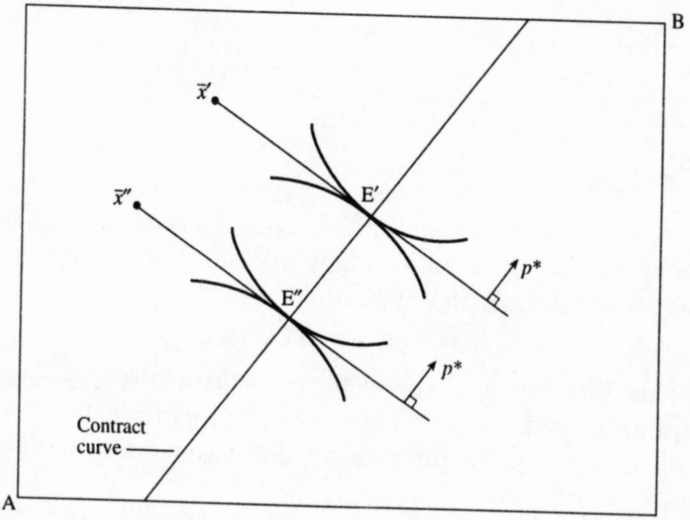

Fig. 2.6

Note: Under consumer aggregation notice that relative prices do not change when there is a redistribution of endowments between A and B. The reason for this is simple:

because the conditions imply a representative consumer with quasi-homothetic utility, we get the diagram of a single consumer and an endowment (see Figure 2.7).

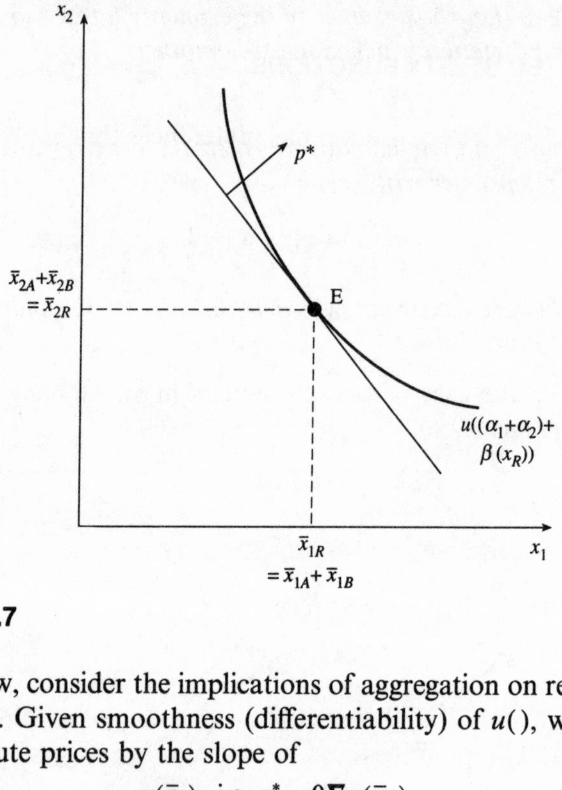

Fig. 2.7

Now, consider the implications of aggregation on relative prices. Given smoothness (differentiability) of $u()$, we can compute prices by the slope of

$$u(\bar{x}_R),\ \text{i.e. } \boldsymbol{p}^* = \theta \nabla \boldsymbol{u}(\bar{\boldsymbol{x}}_R),$$

where $\nabla \boldsymbol{u}$ is the gradient vector of utility at the consumer optimum, and θ is just a constant of proportionality. We will see how this technique is applied with more restrictive utility functions.

SPECIAL UTILITY FUNCTIONS

So far we have assumed that consumers have neoclassical utility functions. But it has been traditional in finance to assume a much more restrictive type of preference that incorporates probabilities and explicit attitudes to risk.

EXPECTED UTILITY FUNCTIONS

Assume that our consumer has preferences that satisfy the expected utility form,

$$U(x_0, x_1, \ldots, x_s) = \sum_{s=1}^{S} u(x_0, x_s)\pi_s,$$

where

$$\pi_s \geqslant 0; \sum_s \pi_s = 1 \text{ and } u(\,) \text{ is neoclassical.}$$

Clearly π_s is a probability of state s; and the consumer evaluates contingent bundles according to 'expected utility'.

Often this utility function is restricted further to be additive-separable over time (as well as over states), i.e.

$$\sum_{s=1}^{S} u(x_0, x_s)\pi_s = u(x_0) + \sum_{s=1}^{S} u(x_s)\pi_s,$$

where $u'(\,) > 0$, and $u''(\,) \leqslant 0$.

Given this set of preferences we can show conditions on $u(\,)$ that will imply neoclassical indifference curves.

THEOREM. *Given $u(\,)$ is strictly increasing and concave, then the preferred sets are convex.*

Proof. Milne (1974).

By using a quadrant diagram (Figure 2.8), we can illustrate this result. Given any point on the constant expected utility locus in the south-west quadrant, we can trace through to its commodity bundle in the north-east quadrant. Thus we can trace out an indifference curve in the contingent commodity quadrant. Notice that it inherits the familiar neoclassical shape.

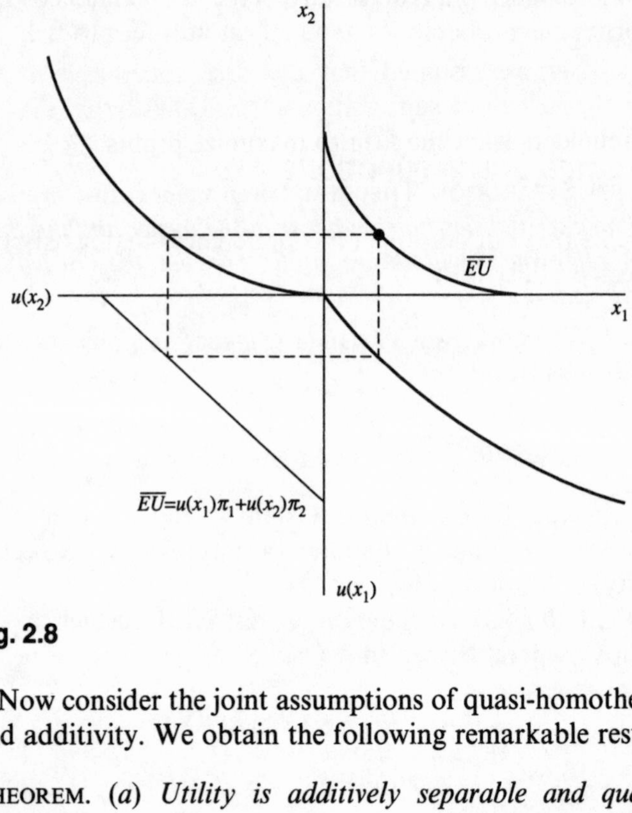

Fig. 2.8

Now consider the joint assumptions of quasi-homotheity and additivity. We obtain the following remarkable result.

THEOREM. (*a*) *Utility is additively separable and quasi-homothetic.*

(*b*)
$$u(x_i) = \begin{cases} \delta(x_s + \alpha_i)^c & \text{for} \quad 0 < c < 1, \\ \lambda \ln(\delta x_s + \alpha_i), & \alpha_i > 0. \\ \lambda \exp(\delta x_s), & \lambda < 0;\ \delta < 0. \end{cases}$$

Statement (*a*) is equivalent to statement (*b*).

Proof. Milne (1979), Brennan and Kraus (1976).

This theorem is important, because it reveals, in conjunction with the representative consumer theorem, the importance of log, power, and exponential utility in creating a representative consumer. We shall see variations on this theorem throughout this book.

WHY DO FIRMS MAXIMIZE PROFIT?

Previously we assumed that the firm maximized profit. Here we will show sufficient conditions that imply that all shareholders want the firm to maximize profits.

FISHER SEPARATION THEOREM *Given competitive markets and no externalities flowing between the owner and the firm, then all owners will desire profit (or net present value) maximization.*

Proof. We know from Varian (1992) that the consumer has an indirect utility function

$$V_i(\boldsymbol{p}^*, W_{0i}),$$

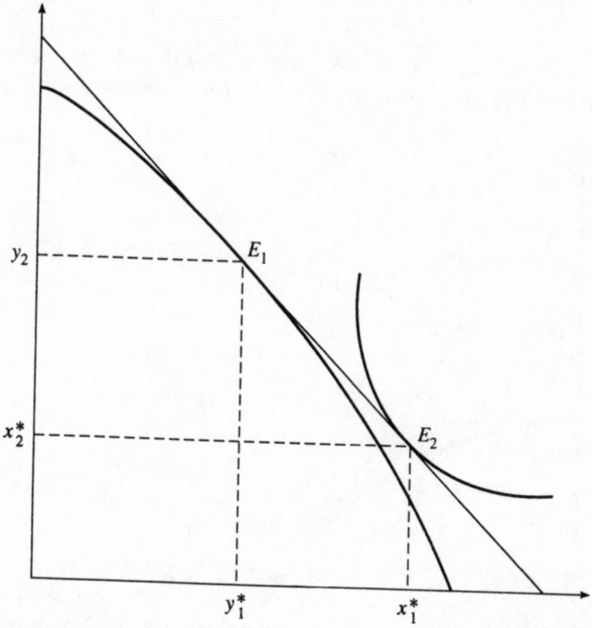

Fig. 2.9

Notes: (1) E_1 is the profit-maximizing production plan (y_1^*, y_2^*).
(2) E_2 is the utility-maximizing consumption plan (x_1^*, x_2^*).

which is strictly increasing in W_{0i}. Because

$$W_{0i} = p^* \bar{x}_i + \sum_j \theta_{ij} p^* y_j \left(1 \geqslant \theta_{ij} \geqslant 0; \sum_j \theta_{ij} = 1\right)$$

then each consumer (with $\theta_{ij} > 0$) prefers y_j^* to any other $y_j \in Y_j$ if $p^* y_j^* \geqslant p^* y_j$.

The Fisher theorem can be illustrated with a simple two-commodity diagram, showing that an owner will want her wealth (or share of profits) to be as large as possible (Figure 2.9).

FAILURE OF THE FISHER THEOREM

It is not difficult to show that without the two assumptions, the Fisher theorem can fail, and owners will disagree

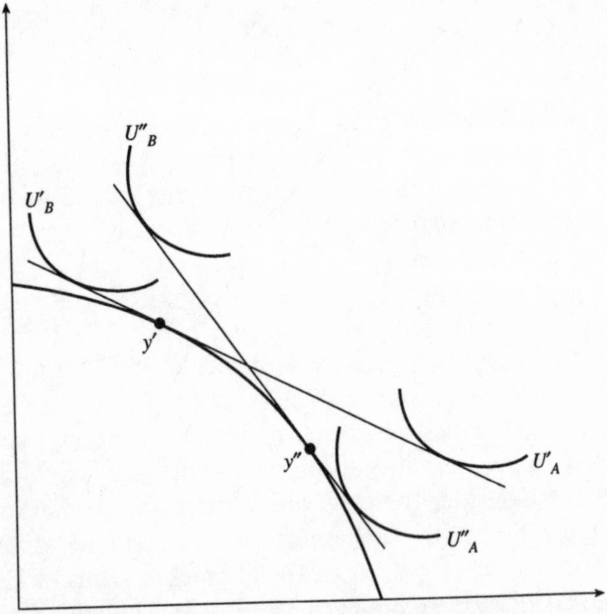

Fig. 2.10

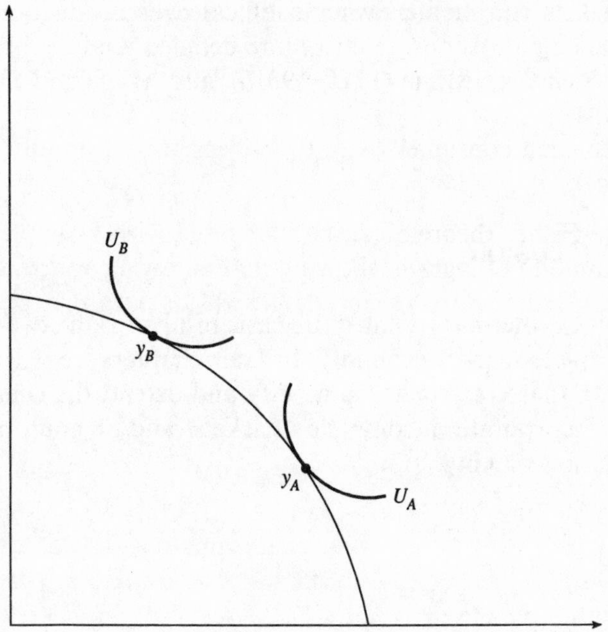

Fig. 2.11

over the production plan. Consider the case where there are two owners with 50 per cent ownership of the technology. Assume that the firm has monopoly power such that for production plan y' there is an associated price vector $p' = p(y')$; and for plan y'' there is a price vector $p'' = p(y'')$. In Figure 2.10 we illustrate how consumer A and consumer B will rank the two plans differently and disagree over which production plan to implement.

A similar conclusion can be reached if there are externalities flowing between the firm and the owners. A special case of an externality occurs when there are missing markets. Consider the case where there are no markets at all. Given the two consumers, A and B, with different preferences, we can illustrate the conflict in terms of Figure 2.11. Consumer A chooses production bundle y_A; and consumer B chooses production $y_B \neq y_A$. Clearly, missing markets can create owner conflicts over production and financing decisions. (For a more detailed analysis of these problems see Milne (1975, 1981*b*), and Milne and Shefrin (1984).)

CONCLUSION

This chapter has outlined the basic results for the two-date, complete market economy. In later chapters we will draw upon these results as we modify and extend the economy to incorporate incomplete markets and/or multiperiod decision-making.

3

Incomplete Markets with Production

Our first modification towards reality is to realize that we do not see a complete set of markets. There are reasons why we do not see markets for some states of the world. One example is the existence of transaction costs in operating markets. For the moment we will not model these costs explicitly, but just assume that certain asset markets exist, and some do not. (A more complete theory would incorporate transaction costs and deduce market activity endogenously.)

THE BASIC MODEL

Consider a set of assets $k = 1, \ldots, K$ with pay-offs $\boldsymbol{Z}_1, \ldots, \boldsymbol{Z}_K$ where $\boldsymbol{Z}_k \in \mathbb{R}^S$. We present two examples of asset pay-offs when there are three states of the world. Assume that the states are ordered according to economic activity such that s_1 is high activity, s_2 is moderate activity, and s_3 is a recession.

	Riskless bond	Equity
$s = 1$	1	3
2	1	2
3	1	1

THE CONSUMER

At time $t = 0$, the consumer buys a_k units of asset k, at prices p_k; and x_{0i} units of the consumption good at price p_0.

At date $t = 1$, the consumer's contingent consumption is constrained by the contingent endowment ($\bar{x}_s$) and the pay-offs for the portfolio, i.e.

$$x_{si} = \sum_{k=1}^{K} Z_{sk} a_{ki} + \bar{x}_{si}, \qquad s = 1, \ldots, S.$$

Now given the consumer's utility function

$$U_i(x_{0i}, x_{1i}, \ldots, x_{Si})$$

the consumer's problem can be written as:

$$\begin{aligned} &\underset{\{x_i \geqslant 0\}}{\text{Max}} \ U_i(x_{0i}, x_{1i}, \ldots, x_{Si}) \\ &s.t. \quad x_{si} = \sum_{k=1}^{K} Z_{sk} a_{ki} + \bar{x}_{si}, \qquad s = 1, \ldots, S \\ &\qquad p_0 x_{0i} + \sum_{k=1}^{K} p_k a_{ki} = W_{0i} \\ &\qquad a_{kj} \geqslant 0 \quad \forall k. \end{aligned} \tag{3.1}$$

Note that the non-negative constraint on asset holdings eliminates borrowing or short sales. Later in the chapter we will explore relaxing this constraint.

We can rewrite the problem, by eliminating the contingent consumption constraints to obtain:

$$\begin{aligned} &\underset{\{x_{0i}, \boldsymbol{a}_i) \geqslant 0\}}{\text{Max}} \ V_i(x_{0i}; \boldsymbol{a}_i) \\ &s.t. \quad p_0 x_{0i} + \sum_k p_k a_{ki} = W_{0i} \end{aligned} \tag{3.2}$$

where (*a*) $V_i(x_{0i}; \boldsymbol{a}_i) \equiv U_i\left(x_{0i}; \left(\sum_k Z_{sk} a_{ki}\right)\right)$, and

(*b*) $(x_{0i}, \boldsymbol{a}_i) \in X_i^A \equiv \mathbb{R}_+^{K+1}$.

Now we can prove the following theorem.

THEOREM 3.1. *Given $U_i()$ is continuous, differentiable, quasi-concave, and strictly increasing, i.e. it is neoclassical, $Z_{sk} \geqslant 0$ and Z_k has at least one strictly positive component; then $V_i()$ is continuous, differentiable, quasi-concave, and strictly increasing.*

Proof. See Milne (1976) Lemma 1, or Milne (1988) Lemmas 1, 2.

This result derives induced preferences over $t = 0$ consumption, and the asset portfolio $\boldsymbol{a}_i$, such that the utility function inherits the standard neoclassical properties. As a consequence all the standard results of consumer theory (Slutsky, etc.) can be used on the consumer portfolio problem.

THE PRODUCER'S PROBLEM

By similar methods we can construct an induced producer's problem over first-date input and asset sales. (We rule out, for the moment, the possibility of the firm holding the assets of other firms.)

The basic firm problem is:

$$\begin{aligned} &\text{Max} \sum_k p_k a_{kj} - p_0 y_{0j} \\ &s.t. \sum_k Z_{sk} a_{kj} = y_{sj}, \qquad s = 1, \ldots, S. \\ &(y_{0j}; y_{ij}, \ldots, y_{sj}) \in Y_j, \\ &a_{kj} \geqslant 0, \forall k. \end{aligned} \tag{3.3}$$

Now, by substituting for y_{sj}, we obtain:

$$\begin{aligned} &\text{Max} \sum_k p_k a_{kj} - p_0 y_{0j} \\ &s.t. \left(y_{0j}; \left(\sum_k Z_{sk} a_{kj} \right) \right) \in Y_j \end{aligned} \tag{3.4}$$

$$a_{kj} \geqslant 0, \forall k.$$

Analogous to the induced-preference argument for the consumer, we can construct an induced asset-production set for the producer:

$$Y_j^A \equiv \{(y_{0j}; \boldsymbol{a}_j) \, \varepsilon \mathbb{R}^{1+K} \,|\, \boldsymbol{y}_j \in Y_j; \, y_{sj} = \sum_k Z_{sk} a_{kj}; \, a_{kj} \geqslant 0, \forall k\}.$$

THEOREM 3.2. *Given Y_j is closed, convex, and $0 \in Y_j$; then Y_j^A is closed, convex and $0 \in Y_j^A$.*

Proof. See Milne (1976) Lemma 2.

Thus the firm's problem collapses to the neoclassical form (assuming a differentiable production function).

$$\begin{aligned} &\text{Max} \sum_k p_k a_{kj} - p_0 y_{0j} \\ &s.t. \quad (y_{0j}, \boldsymbol{a}_j) \in Y_j^A. \end{aligned} \tag{3.5}$$

Again, standard neoclassical techniques of comparative statics can be applied to the firm's problem. To close the model, we assume the commodity and asset markets clear.

DEFINITION 3.1. *A competitive equilibrium for an incomplete asset economy is a price vector*

$$(p_0^*, p_1^*, \ldots, p_K^*)$$

and an allocation

$$((x_{0i}^*; \boldsymbol{a}_i^*) \forall i; \, (y_{0j}^*; \boldsymbol{a}_j^*) \forall j)$$

such that

(*a*) $(x_{0i}^*; \boldsymbol{a}_i^*)$ *is the solution to the consumer's problem* (3.2);

(*b*) $(y_{0j}^*; \boldsymbol{a}_j^*)$ *is the solution to the producer's problem* (3.3);

(*c*) $\left[\begin{aligned} &\sum_i x_{0i}^* = \sum_i \bar{x}_{0i} + \sum_j y_{0j}^*; \\ &\sum_i \boldsymbol{a}_i^* = \sum_j \boldsymbol{a}_j^*. \end{aligned}\right.$

EXISTENCE OF EQUILIBRIUM

Given that the reduced-form asset economy has the same structure as the standard Debreu economy, then it is easy to modify the standard existence proofs. If we allow short sales/borrowing, then there are some complexities. We will deal with these shortly.

OPTIMALITY AND THE WELFARE THEOREMS

With the Arrow–Debreu complete market model we know that the equilibrium is Pareto optimal. But with incomplete markets this is no longer true. Nevertheless, for the single commodity/two-date model we can define the concept of a constrained optimum that is due to Diamond (1967). The trick is define an optimum in terms of our asset economy.

DEFINITION 3.2. *Given a set of consumers*

$$\{(V_i(); X_i^A; \bar{\boldsymbol{x}}_i)\}$$

and a set of producers $\{Y_j^A\}$ *then a constrained optimal allocation*

$$\{(x_{0i}^*, \boldsymbol{a}_i^*); (y_{0j}^*, \boldsymbol{a}_j^*)\}$$

is a feasible allocation for which there exists no other feasible allocation

$$\{(x_{0i}', \boldsymbol{a}_i'); (y_{0j}', \boldsymbol{a}_j')$$

for which

$$V_i(x_{0i}', \boldsymbol{a}_i') \geqslant V_i(x_{0i}^*, \boldsymbol{x}_i^*)$$

for each i and with strict inequality for at least one consumer.

Notice that the set of feasible allocations is constrained by the set of asset returns $[\boldsymbol{Z}_1, \ldots, \boldsymbol{Z}_K]$ which is treated as a 'technology' in the construction of

$$V_i(); X_i^A; \text{ and } Y_j^A.$$

Now by using standard techniques, we can prove the two fundamental theorems for our reduced-form asset economy. (For proofs based on Debreu see Milne, 1988.)

THE FISHER SEPARATION THEOREM IN THE ASSET ECONOMY

Given that the reduced-form asset economy has the same structure as an Arrow–Debreu economy we can simply adapt the proof of the Fisher separation theorem to our new economy by relabelling variables. Clearly all owners will want the firm to maximize profit, if they are initial shareholders of the firm. Notice that if the firm introduced an asset with returns that were not included in the current set of assets (or a linear combination of the current set) then it would be a monopolist, and the Fisher theorem fails. For more on this see Milne (1976) (on leverage) or Milne and Shefrin (1984) (for production decisions).

Indeed with non-competitive behaviour and/or externalities there may be no constitution for the firm (see Milne, 1981*b*).

INTRODUCING SHORT-SELLING AND BORROWING

So far we have avoided discussing short-selling and borrowing, by constraining the consumer's asset purchases to $\mathbb{R}_+^K$, and the firm's asset issuing to $\mathbb{R}_+^K$.

We can extend the analysis to allow for short-selling by consumers and firms. This introduces some additional complications that we will address here briefly. To keep the argument as simple as possible, we restrict our discussion to an exchange economy with only two consumers. (The general economy is discussed in Milne, 1976 and 1980.)

Consider two consumers $i = A, B$, with consumer problems with unlimited short-selling:

$$\text{Max } U_i(x_{1i}, \ldots, x_{Si})$$

$$s.t. \quad x_{Si} = \sum_{k=1}^{K} Z_{sk} a_{ki}, \qquad S = 1, \ldots, S;$$

$$\sum_k p_k a_{ki} = \sum_k p_k \bar{a}_{ki}.$$

For simplicity we have ignored $t = 0$ consumption, and introduced endowments of the assets.

For illustrative purposes, consider just two assets, i.e. $K = 2$. We can now draw an Edgeworth box. Assuming no short-sales, the old constraints are represented by the dashed box so that short-sales are outside the dashed box. In Figure 3.1, the equilibrium allocation E is outside the box. After asset trades, consumer A is long in both assets, but consumer B is long in asset 2 but short in asset 1.

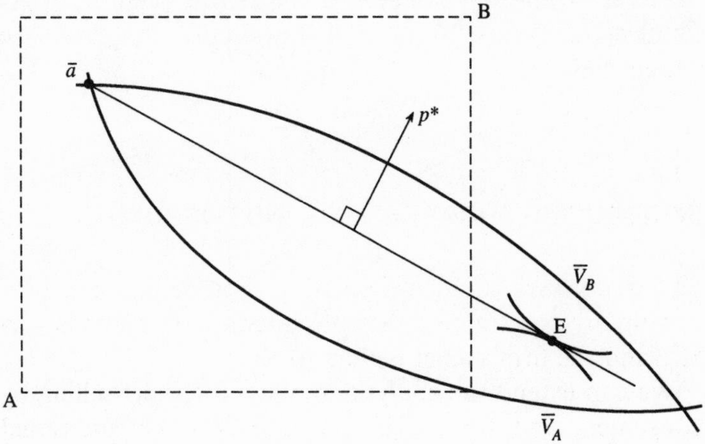

Fig. 3.1

So long as the induced gains from trade line is bounded (it is closed, clearly) then we do not run into any problems in proving the existence of an equilibrium. (For a proof along these lines see Hart, 1974, or more recently Werner, 1987.)

But there are examples where such a proof fails. For example, consider the case where both consumers are risk-neutral, but have different probability distributions. In general, this will imply different slopes for their linear-induced preferences over assets.

We can check that there will be no equilibrium in this economy. If we postulate a price vector $\boldsymbol{p}'$ and an allocation E', both consumers will wish to trade away from E'—a contradiction. This will be true for any postulated price $\boldsymbol{p}'$ that has a price line in the gains from trade cone $\bar{V}_B \bar{a} \bar{V}_A$. Does this imply that there is no equilibrium for an economy with risk-neutral consumers, different expectations, and short-selling?

A possible solution to this problem is to recall the underlying constraints on contingent consumption, and see if they impose constraints on the asset-constraint sets that will bound the asset economy.

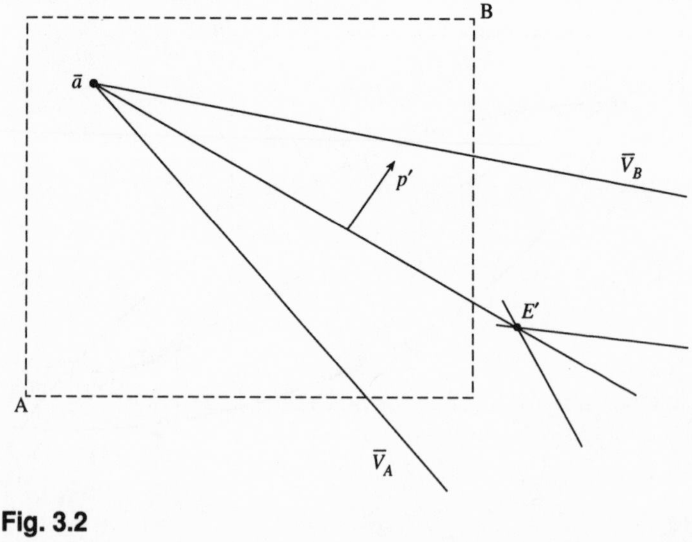

Fig. 3.2

Intuitively, unbounded short-selling involves consumers believing that there is unbounded contingent consumption in at least one state of the world. This assertion follows directly from the observation that any allocation sequence where the consumer is increasingly better off, must imply increasing contingent consumption. (For a more detailed discussion see Milne, 1980.)

Thus, if we define asset constraint sets,

$$A_i = \{\boldsymbol{a}_i \in \mathbb{R}^K \mid \boldsymbol{x}_i \in X_i;\ x_{si} = \sum_k Z_{sk} a_{ki}\}$$

and assume that $\boldsymbol{Z}_1, \ldots, \boldsymbol{Z}_K$ is of rank K, then standard constructions of feasible asset trades will imply that the set of obtainable allocations is compact, and standard existence proofs can be used (see Milne 1976, 1980). Consider the example shown in Figure 3.3.

MORE GENERAL CONTINGENT COMMODITY SPACES'

For the sake of simplicity, we have restricted the contingent commodity space to be $\mathbb{R}^S$. But the construction of

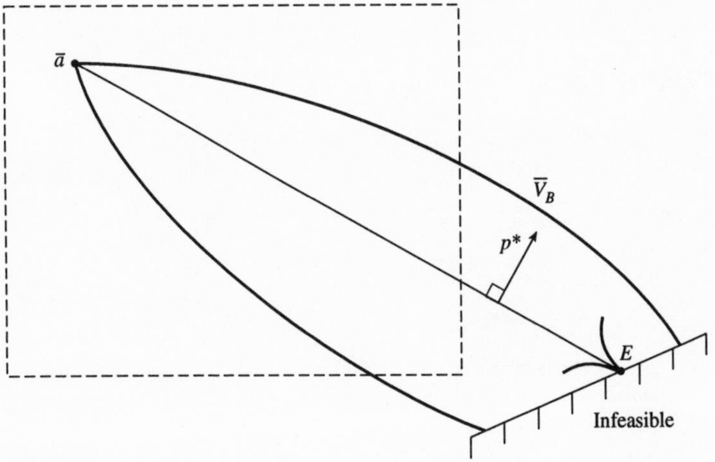

Fig. 3.3

induced preferences is sufficiently flexible for it to be extended to deal with infinite-dimensional contingent commodity spaces. Because such an extension requires more complex mathematics, we will omit any formal analysis and direct the reader to Milne (1981*a*, 1988) for a more complete discussion.

CONCLUSION

In this chapter we have introduced incomplete asset markets and explored some basic results concerning an equilibrium and its optimality properties. In the next chapter, we will begin our discussion of asset-pricing methods by introducing arbitrage pricing using our construction of induced preferences and induced-production sets.

4

Arbitrage and Asset-Pricing: Induced-Preference Approach

Given the basic asset economy outlined in the last chapter, we can now analyse the role of arbitrage in asset allocations and asset prices. By using induced preferences, we have a simple tool for constructing geometric proofs. In this chapter, we will illustrate the ideas using examples, but the ideas generalize in a straightforward fashion (see Milne, 1981*a*, 1988).

Consider an economy where asset 1 has contingent returns that are a linear combination of the asset returns of $k = 2, \ldots, K$, i.e.

$$\boldsymbol{Z}_1 = \sum_{k=2}^{K} \alpha_k \boldsymbol{Z}_k \text{ for non-trival } \{\alpha_k\}.$$

Assume that $\boldsymbol{Z}_2, \ldots, \boldsymbol{Z}_K$ are linearly independent. Define

$$\boldsymbol{Z}_P = \sum_{k=2}^{K} \alpha_k \boldsymbol{Z}_k$$

to be the returns on a portfolio with returns that are identical to $\boldsymbol{Z}_1$.

Consider a consumer at an optimum i.e.

$$(x_{0i}^*, a_i^*) \quad \text{solves} \quad \left[\begin{array}{l} \text{Max } V_i(x_{0i}, \boldsymbol{a}_i) \\ s.t.\ p_0 x_{0i} + \sum p_k a_{ki} = W_{0i}. \end{array} \right.$$

At the optimal $(x_{0i}^*, \boldsymbol{a}_i^*)$ the indifference surface in asset spaces will be defined by:

$$S_i^* \equiv \{a_i \in \mathbb{R}^K \mid V_i(x_{0i}^*, \boldsymbol{a}_i^*) = \bar{V}_i\}.$$

By construction it will contain the linear manifold defined by

$$\alpha_1 \boldsymbol{Z}_1 - \sum_{k=2}^{K} \alpha_k \boldsymbol{Z}_k = 0,$$

which is independent of the neoclassical utility function $U_i()$. The reader can check this assertion by calculating the marginal rate of substitution between the portfolio and asset 1, given that $U_i()$ and $V_i()$ are differentiable. But we can dispense with differentiability of $U_i()$, and the indifference manifold S_i^* will still exist. Thus differentiable utility is not necessary for our argument. In other words, if we project down on to the asset subspace we will obtain a linear indifference curve over asset 1, and the composite portfolio $(\alpha_2, \ldots, \alpha_K)$ (see Figure 4.1).

If the asset prices of asset 1 and assets 2, . . . , K are *not* in the relation

$$p_1 = \sum_{k=2}^{K} \alpha_k p_k$$

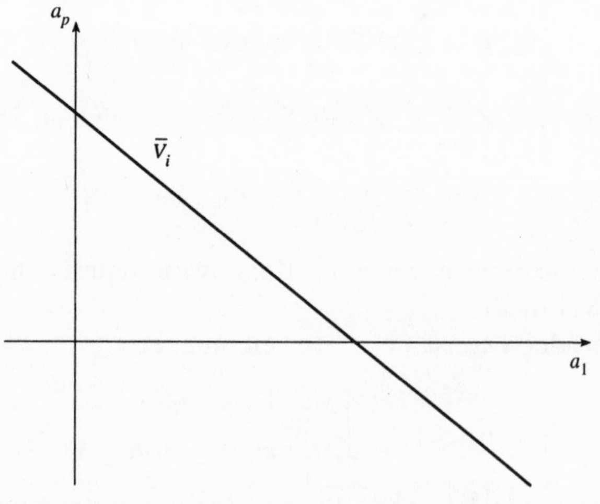

Fig. 4.1

then the consumer will want to take unbounded trades, violating the assumption of a consumer optimum. This is illustrated in Figure 4.2, where the consumer will hold increasingly larger amounts of asset 1 and short-sell the portfolio. This is the case where

$$p_1 < \sum_{k=2}^{K} \alpha_k p_k.$$

With the reverse inequality the consumer will want to take the opposite position. Notice that the consumer will not be constrained in the contingent commodity space by such trades, because their impact is zero, as a perfect hedge (see Figure 4.2).

The only configuration of asset prices consistent with a consumer optimum is where

$$p_1 = \sum_{k=2}^{K} \alpha_k p_k.$$

This price relation is known as an arbitrage (free) pricing relation. To summarize:

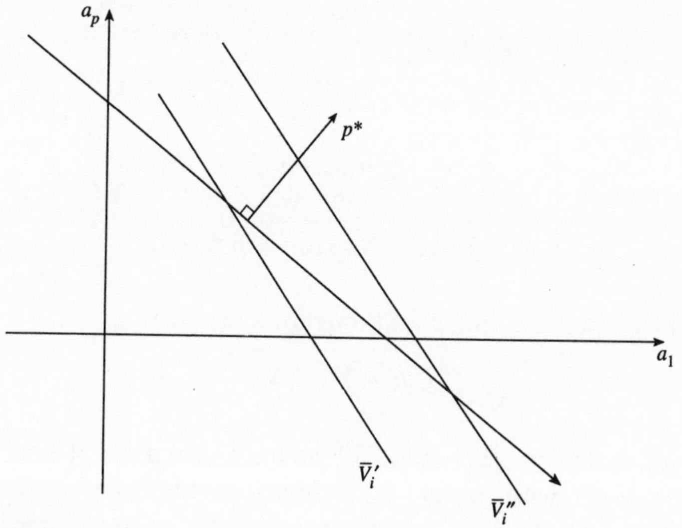

Fig. 4.2

THEOREM 4.1. *If the asset returns are linearly dependent, i.e. there exists non-trivial* $\{\alpha_k\}$ *such that*

$$\sum_k \alpha_k \boldsymbol{Z}_k = 0,$$

then the absence of arbitrage and short-selling constraints implies

$$\sum_k \alpha_k p_k = 0.$$

Having deduced restrictions on prices, we turn now to consider the non-uniqueness of asset allocations, when there is linear dependence on future asset returns.

Consider an equilibrium where Theorem 4.1 holds. An allocation for this economy will be

$$[(x^*_{0i}, \boldsymbol{a}^*_i)\forall i, (y^*_{0j}, \boldsymbol{a}^*_j)\forall j].$$

The opportunity sets of the consumers and firms can be written as

$$x^*_{si} = \sum_k Z_{sk} a^*_{ki} \ \forall s$$

$$p_0 x_{0i} + \sum_k p_k a^*_{ki} = W_{0i} \quad \text{for each consumer } i,$$

and

$$\pi^*_j = \sum_k p_k a_{kj} - p_0 y^*_{0j}$$

$$y^*_{sj} = \sum_k Z_{sk} a^*_{kj} \ \forall s \quad \text{for each firm } j.$$

The market-clearing conditions for asset, are

$$\sum_i a^*_{ki} = \sum_j a^*_{kj}, \ \forall k.$$

Notice that in asset space $\mathbb{R}^K$ we have here a set of linear equations with linear dependence in the asset return $\{Z_{sk}\}$ and, by arbitrage (free) pricing, the same linear dependence in the asset prices. It is an easy exercise in linear algebra to prove that there is a linear subspace of asset allocations that solve the opportunity set/market-clearing system, and gives a constant contingent consumption/production allocation

$$[(\boldsymbol{x}_i^*)\forall i;\ (\boldsymbol{y}_j^*)\forall j].$$

For details of the proof, see Milne (1988).

The intuition of this result can be illustrated by an exchange economy, unbounded Edgeworth box. Consumers A and B have parallel indifference curves through the asset endowment $\bar{\boldsymbol{a}}$. The asset prices $\boldsymbol{p}^*$ will be determined by arbitrage, i.e. orthogonal to the linear indifference curves (see Figure 4.3).

Notice that the result can be obtained for the case with short-selling constraints, except that the equilibrium asset allocation is a subset of the linear manifold, defined by the short-selling constraints. In Figure 4.3 this would be all the asset allocations on the line segment αβ.

In the case of a production economy, we can illustrate the result with a simple consumer/firm diagram (see Figure 4.4). In this Figure the consumer and firm can take

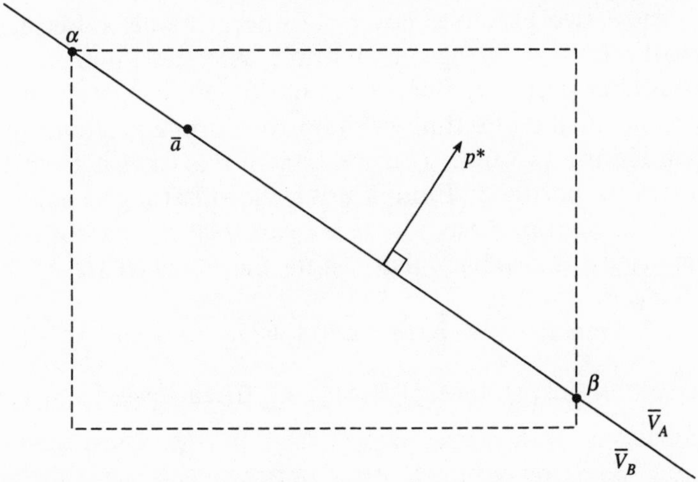

Fig. 4.3

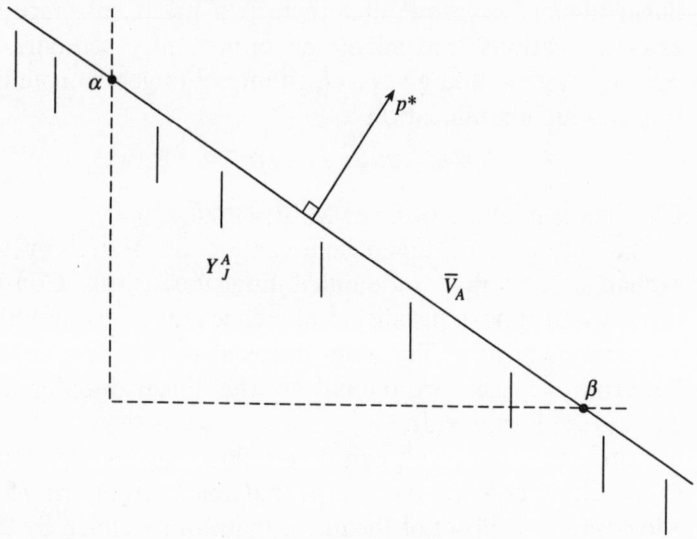

Fig. 4.4

offsetting asset positions to each other to obtain the same contingent consumption/production plans. Notice that the constrained short-selling result obtains here also on the segment αβ.

These two examples cover consumers taking offsetting positions to a change in a firm's asset portfolio, or a consumer portfolio. But we can illustrate the case where a firm takes the offsetting position to a firm's portfolio by considering two firms (Figure 4.5). In this case, if Firm 1 alters its portfolio, Firm 2 takes the offsetting position. Indeed, if Firm 2 has $y_1^* = 0$, we can treat it as a costless financial intermediary that offsets the financial structure change of Firm 1.

To summarize, we have the following theorem:

THEOREM 4.2 (MODIGLIANI–MILLER). *Given dependent asset returns*

i.e. $\exists$ *non-trivial* $\{\alpha_k\}$ *such that* $\sum_k \alpha_k \boldsymbol{Z}_k = 0$

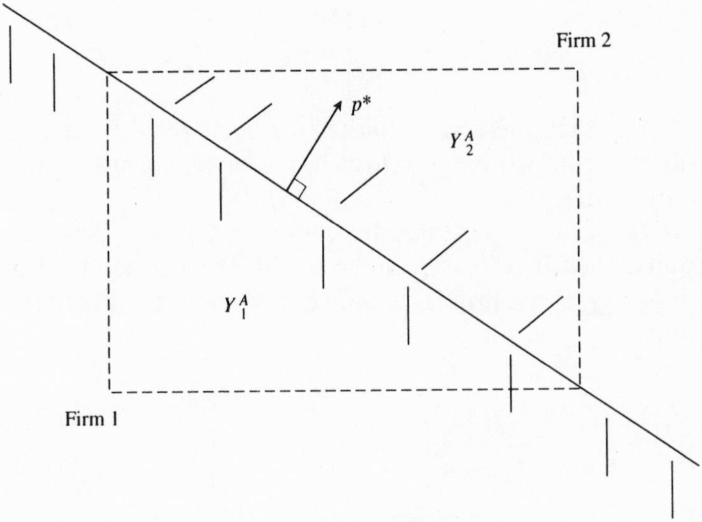

Fig. 4.5

then in equilibrium

$$\sum_k \alpha_k p_k = 0;$$

and there is a linear manifold of equilibrium asset allocations over which all agents are indifferent.

We called this theorem the Modigliani–Miller (1958) theorem because it expresses the central idea of that famous paper. For a discussion of the evolution of the theorem and its applications see Miller (1988).

To illustrate the power of the Modigliani–Miller theorem, we consider two examples.

1. Firm Leverage with Default Risk

Consider Firm 1 to have unlevered equity with pay-off per share of:

$$\begin{array}{c} \\ s=1 \\ 2 \\ 3 \end{array} \overset{\boldsymbol{Z}_E}{\begin{bmatrix} 10 \\ 6 \\ 4 \end{bmatrix}}.$$

Given that there is a market for such pay-off streams which is competitive, the firm has a current market price of its shares p_E.

If the firm restructures by choosing to issue debt *and* equity, then it will retire some of the existing equity. For simplicity let the firm issue only one share of the unlevered equity.

$$\begin{array}{c} s=1 \\ 2 \\ 3 \end{array} \quad \overset{\boldsymbol{Z}_E}{\begin{bmatrix} 10 \\ 6 \\ 4 \end{bmatrix}} \, 1 = \overset{\boldsymbol{Z}_L}{\begin{bmatrix} 6 \\ 2 \\ 0 \end{bmatrix}} \, 1 + \overset{\boldsymbol{Z}_B}{\begin{bmatrix} 1 \\ 1 \\ 1 \end{bmatrix}} \, 4.$$

Unlevered equity   *Levered equity*   *Riskless debt*

In the new structure, the firm has issued four bonds and one new levered share.

Given competitive markets for the unlevered shares, and the riskless bond, the levered share pay-off can be replicated: i.e. $\boldsymbol{Z}_L = \boldsymbol{Z}_E - \boldsymbol{Z}_B.4$.

By the Modigliani–Miller theorem we have:

(i) $p_L = p_E - p_B.4$.

(ii) All agents are indifferent to the financial restructuring as they can take offsetting asset allocations. We can extend the example to allow for default risk.

$$\begin{array}{c} s=1 \\ 2 \\ 3 \end{array} \quad \overset{\boldsymbol{Z}_E}{\begin{bmatrix} 10 \\ 6 \\ 4 \end{bmatrix}} \, 1 = \overset{\boldsymbol{Z}_L}{\begin{bmatrix} 5 \\ 1 \\ 0 \end{bmatrix}} \, 1 + \overset{\boldsymbol{Z}_{DB}}{\begin{bmatrix} 1 \\ 1 \\ 4/5 \end{bmatrix}} \, 5.$$

In this case, the firm has issued five bonds; and in state 3 the firm's bond commitments exceed its cash flow, and it defaults. The bond-holders divide up the cash flow earning only 4/5 of the face value.

So long as there is a competitive market for this defaulting bond (i.e. there is a competitive market for this cash flow) then Modigliani–Miller applies and:

(i) $p_L = p_E - p_{DB}5$.

(ii) All agents are indifferent to the financial restructuring.

It is important to realize that if the firm changes its financial structure, and creates a security that is not traded or 'spanned' by the original assets, then the firm is a monopolist, who perturbs the whole equilibrium. That is, the Fisher separation and Modigliani–Miller theorems fail. (For more on this see Milne, 1975 and 1981*a*, Milne and Shefrin, 1984.)

2. Call Option Pricing

Consider the two-date model introduced by Cox, Ross, and Rubinstein (1979). Let there be two states of the world, and two securities: a stock and a riskless bond:

$$\begin{array}{cc} & \boldsymbol{Z}_S \quad \boldsymbol{Z}_B \\ s = \begin{array}{c} 1 \\ 2 \end{array} & \begin{bmatrix} up_S \\ dp_S \end{bmatrix} \begin{bmatrix} R \\ R \end{bmatrix}. \end{array}$$

The current price of the stock is p_S and in state 1 the stock can go 'up' in price to give up_S; and in state 2 it can go 'down' in price to dp_S. The return to the bond (current price $p_B = 1$) is $R \equiv (1 + r)$ in both states of the world. Let r be the rate of interest. To avoid arbitrage possibilities, we require $u > R > d$.

Notice that there are two securities and only two states of the world. In simple linear algebra terms, the asset returns span the states of the world. Given that the asset returns span the states, we can create two portfolios that have primitive Arrow–Debreu security returns. That is:

$$\begin{array}{cc} & \textbf{\textit{AD1}} & & \textbf{\textit{S}} & & \textbf{\textit{B}} \\ s = 1 & \begin{bmatrix} 1 \\ 0 \end{bmatrix} & = & \begin{bmatrix} up_S \\ dp_S \end{bmatrix} & [p_s(u-d)]^{-1} - & \begin{bmatrix} R \\ R \end{bmatrix} & d[R(u-d)]^{-1}. \\ 2 & & & & & & \end{array}$$

The replicating portfolio for this asset takes

$$[p_S(u-d)]^{-1}$$

units of the stock; and borrows

$$d.[R(u-d)]^{-1}$$

units of the bond. By the Modigliani–Miller theorem, we can price *AD1* by arbitrage, and the introduction of the *AD1* security is a matter of indifference to all agents.

If the price of *AD1* is p_{AD1}, then by arbitrage:

$$\begin{aligned} p_{AD1} &= p_S[p_S(u-d)]^{-1} - 1.d[R(u-d)]^{-1} \\ &= [u-d]^{-1}[1 - d.R^{-1}] \\ &= (1+r)^{-1}\left[\frac{(1+r)-d}{u-d}\right]. \end{aligned}$$

By similar reasoning, we can create the second Arrow–Debreu security:

$$\begin{array}{cc} & \textbf{\textit{AD2}} & & \textbf{\textit{S}} & & \textbf{\textit{B}} \\ s = 1 & \begin{bmatrix} 0 \\ 1 \end{bmatrix} & = - & \begin{bmatrix} up_S \\ dp_S \end{bmatrix} & [p_s(u-d)]^{-1} + & \begin{bmatrix} R \\ R \end{bmatrix} & u[(u-d)R]^{-1}. \\ 2 & & & & & & \end{array}$$

By arbitrage:

$$\begin{aligned} p_{AD2} &= -p_S[p_S(u-d)]^{-1} + 1u.[(u-d)R]^{-1} \\ &= (1+r)^{-1}\left[\frac{u-(1+r)}{u-d}\right]. \end{aligned}$$

Observe the symmetry in the Arrow–Debreu prices. First they involve a present-value term $(1+r)^{-1}$, and then an undiscounted term in square brackets. By construction both prices are strictly positive. Furthermore, observe that

$$p_{AD1} + p_{AD2} = (1 + r)^{-1}\left[\frac{(1 + r) - d + u - (1 + r)}{u - d}\right]$$

$$= (1 + r)^{-1}.$$

In words, a simple portfolio of one *AD1* and one *AD2*, will have a current market value (by arbitrage) of $(1 + r)^{-1}$. After all, the portfolio has the same pay-off as a riskless bond. Using the device of creating replicating portfolios one can price any asset by arbitrage. For example, consider a call option on a stock. Given the strike price K such that $up_s > K > 0$, the option will be exercised in $s = 1$, and will lapse in $s = 2$. The call's pay-off is given by:

$$\begin{matrix} s = 1 \\ 2 \end{matrix}\begin{bmatrix} up_S - K \\ 0 \end{bmatrix}.$$

By arbitrage, we can price the call:

$$p_{C0} = [up_S - K]p^*_{AD1} = [up_S - K](1 + r)^{-1}\frac{[1 + r - d]}{u - d}$$

$$= (1 + r)^{-1}\left[p_S\left[\frac{u(1 + r - d)}{u - d}\right] - \frac{K(1 + r - d)}{u - d}\right].$$

Notice that the call option has been priced in two stages: (i) by replicating Arrow–Debreu securities; (ii) by replicating the option using the Arrow–Debreu securities. But of course, we can collapse both steps into one, and think of the replication in terms of the underlying stock and bond. This is the intuition underlying the binomial option pricing model, and its continuous time counterpart, the Black–Scholes (1973) option pricing model.

COMPLETE ASSET MARKETS

The call option example suggests a more general result: given a set of assets that span the full space of contingent consumption, then we can reproduce Arrow–Debreu securities by forming portfolios of the original securities.

This is formalized in the following extension of Theorem 4.2.

Corollary 4.2.1. Given the matrix of security returns $[\boldsymbol{Z}_1, \ldots, \boldsymbol{Z}_K]$ has rank $S = K$ then there exists a matrix of portfolio holdings $[\alpha_{sk}]$ such that

$$[\boldsymbol{Z}_1, \ldots, \boldsymbol{Z}_K]\,[\alpha_{sk}] = I.$$

Furthermore

$$p_s = \sum_k \alpha_{sk} p_k,$$

and all agents are indifferent to the introduction of the Arrow securities.

Having constructed the Arrow securities from the spanning set of assets, we apply Theorem 4.2 again to value any asset introduced into the economy.

Corollary 4.2.2. Given an asset economy with assets that contain the Arrow–Debreu set, then any asset k introduced into the economy can be priced as

$$p_k = \sum_{s=1}^{S} p_s Z_{sk};$$

and its introduction is a matter of indifference to all agents.

Although these two corollaries appear trivial in a two-date model they can be extended to multidate models (as we will see) to obtain a whole range of derivative asset-pricing formulae.

One last comment: we know from Chapter 2 that an Arrow–Debreu economy with a complete set of Arrow–Debreu securities achieves a Pareto optimal allocation of contingent commodities. By applying Corollary 4.2.1, we know that an economy with an arbitrary set of assets where rank $[\boldsymbol{Z}_1, \ldots, \boldsymbol{Z}_K] = S$ will also have a Pareto optimal allocation of resources.

It is important to observe that complete markets are sufficient for Pareto optimality, but they are not necessary. Consider the following trivial example. Let there be an economy with one consumer with an endowment $\bar{x}_0$ and one asset $\bar{a}_1$. If we set the consumer's optimal choice

$$(x_0^* = \bar{x}_0, \ a_1^* = \bar{a}_i)$$

and have supporting prices (p_0, p_1) for the indifference curve defined by

$$V(\bar{x}_0, \bar{a}_1),$$

then we have constructed a trivial competitive equilibrium. By construction

$$\bar{x}_s = x_s^* = Z_{s1}\, a_1^* = Z_{s1}\, \bar{a}_1, \ \text{for all } s.$$

Given smooth preferences for $U(\,)$ we have supporting prices

$$(p_0, p_1, \ldots, p_S) \quad \text{for } U(\bar{x}_0, \bar{x}_1, \ldots, \bar{x}_s)$$

and this is a trivial competitive equilibrium in the contingent commodity space. By the first fundamental theorem of welfare economics it is a Pareto optimum. In Chapter 6 we will generalize this example to a class of representative agent models, showing that there are two major routes to Pareto optimality in asset economies, spanning and the construction of a representative consumer.

5

Martingale Pricing Methods

An alternative and more popular method for asset-pricing is the so-called martingale pricing or risk-neutral pricing method. The idea is very simple particularly if $U_i()$ is differentiable. The non-differentiable case is treated at the end of this chapter.

Consider the consumers' problem:

$$\operatorname{Max} U_i(x_{0i}; Za_i) \tag{5.1}$$

$$s.t.\quad p_0 x_{0i} + \sum_k p_k a_{ki} = W_{0i}.$$

Assuming $U_i()$ is neoclassical (and differentiable), we obtain the following necessary conditions for an interior maximum:

$$\frac{\partial U_i}{\partial x_{0i}} = \lambda p_0 \tag{5.2a}$$

$$\sum_{s=1}^{S} \frac{\partial U_i}{\partial x_{si}} Z_{sk} = \lambda p_k, \quad k = 1, \ldots, K. \tag{5.2b}$$

Conditions (5.2*b*) can be written more compactly in matrix form:

$$\nabla \boldsymbol{U}_i \boldsymbol{Z} = \lambda \boldsymbol{p} \quad \text{or} \quad \nabla \tilde{\boldsymbol{U}}_i \boldsymbol{Z} = \boldsymbol{p}, \tag{5.3}$$

where $\nabla \boldsymbol{U}_i$ is a vector with components

$$\frac{\partial U_i}{\partial x_{si}};$$

$\nabla \tilde{\boldsymbol{U}}_i$ is a vector with components

$$\frac{\partial U_i}{\partial x_{si}} \cdot \lambda^{-1};$$

and $\boldsymbol{p}$ is the vector of asset prices.

From the strict monotonicity of the utility function, we know that $\nabla U_i \gg 0$ (i.e. all components are strictly positive).

Now let us introduce the following normalization tricks. First define

$$\gamma_i \equiv \sum_{s=1}^{S} \frac{\partial U_i}{\partial x_{si}} \cdot \lambda^{-1};$$

then define

$$q_{si} \equiv \frac{\partial U_i}{\partial x_{si}} \lambda^{-1} \cdot \gamma_i^{-1}.$$

Clearly $q_{si} > 0$, for all s; and

$$\sum_s q_{si} = 1.$$

Thus the normalized marginal utility vector has the same properties as a probability vector. Furthermore γ_i represents the marginal rate of substitution between consumption at $t = 0$ and a vector of unit contingent consumptions. Notice the i subscripts which denote the marginal conditions for the ith consumer.

Returning to condition (5.3), we obtain:

$$\sum_{s=1}^{S} (\gamma_i Z_{sk}) q_{si} = p_k, \qquad k = 1, \ldots, K. \tag{5.4}$$

If we interpret Z_{sk} as the future contingent price of asset k, then (5.4) says that the consumer will optimize, treating the asset prices as a subjectively discounted martingale. (A martingale is a stochastic process where the current value equals the expected future values.)

Given there exists a riskless asset R such that $Z_{sR} = 1$ for all $s = 1, \ldots, S$; and $p_R \equiv (1 + r)^{-1}$, then (5.4) becomes:

$$\sum_{s=1}^{S} (1+r)^{-1} Z_{sk} q_{si} = p_k, \qquad k = 1, \ldots, K. \tag{5.5}$$

The subjective discount rates have been equalized because all consumers face the same riskless asset, and each consumer is at an interior maximum.

Using this technology, we can reproduce our arbitrage pricing results of Chapter 4:

THEOREM 5.1. *Given a set of assets with non-trivial* $\{\alpha_k\}$ *such that*

$$\sum_k \alpha_k \boldsymbol{Z}_k = 0,$$

then

$$\sum_k \alpha_k p_k = 0.$$

Proof. From (5.4)

$$\sum \alpha_k p_k = \sum_k \alpha_k \sum_s \gamma_i Z_{sk} q_{si} = \sum_s \gamma_i \left(\sum_k \alpha_k Z_{sk} \right) q_{si} = 0.$$

Notice that Theorem 5.1 reproduces the result of Theorem 4.1. Of course, we can obtain the same result by considering firm j and deriving γ_j, q_{sj}, as the firm shadow prices on contingent productions. Most theoretical and applied papers and texts ignore the firm, and concentrate on the consumer-optimizing problem, even though arbitrage activity in financial markets is undertaken largely by firms.

RISK-NEUTRAL PRICING?

Given the characterization of asset prices from conditions (5.4) and (5.5), it is tempting to ask: can we exploit the characterization to price assets 'as if' there were risk-neutral consumers? This is false in general. It is true that if all consumers have von Neumann–Morgenstern risk-neutral preferences, then we have:

Lemma 5.1. If all consumers have utility functions

$$U_i(x_i) = u_i(x_{0i}) + \sum_s u_i(x_{si})\pi_s,$$

with

$$u_i(x_{si}) = \alpha + \beta x_{si},$$

then $q_{si} = \pi_s$ and $p_k = \sum_s (1 + r)^{-1} Z_{sk}\pi_s, \quad k = 1, \ldots, K.$

Proof. From the definition $q_{si} = \pi_s$; and the pricing rule follows by direct substitution.

This result fails if consumers had preferences satisfying the Savage axioms and disagreed on the subjective probabilities, i.e. $\pi_{si'} \neq \pi_{si''}$. In this case, we have linear indifference curves and corner solutions to avoid unbounded asset holdings with short-selling.

But without risk-neutrality, the $\boldsymbol{q}_i$ vector may bear little relation to the probabilities $\boldsymbol{\pi}$. For example, if there is a consumer with von Neumann–Morgenstern risk-averse preferences

$$u_i(x_{0i}) + \sum_s u_i(x_{si})\pi_s$$

such that

$$u_i'() > 0, u_i''() < 0,$$

then

$$q_{si}(x_{si}^*) = u_i'(x_{si}^*)\pi_s(\lambda_i \cdot \gamma_i)^{-1}.$$

Clearly probabilities, attitudes to risk and intertemporal substitution are intertwined in the personalized Arrow–Debreu shadow prices. Later we shall see how in various applications further assumptions are introduced to relate all the $\boldsymbol{q}_i$ and $\boldsymbol{\pi}$.

SPANNING, PARETO OPTIMALITY, AND MARTINGALE PRICING

We know from the first fundamental theorem of welfare economics that a competitive equilibrium in an Arrow–

Debreu economy will achieve a Pareto optimal allocation. In Chapter 4, we showed using the induced-preference method that complete asset markets allowed us to construct an Arrow–Debreu set of securities; and that by appealing to the first welfare theorem the allocation was Pareto optimal in contingent commodities.

Here, we will prove essentially the same result using the martingale approach, showing how the personalized prices γ_i, q_i can be characterized in complete asset markets.

THEOREM 5.2 *Given an asset return matrix* $[\boldsymbol{Z}_1, \ldots, \boldsymbol{Z}_K]$ *which spans* $\mathbb{R}^S$, *then the equilibrium allocation will achieve a Pareto optimum in the contingent commodity space; and*

$$\gamma_i = \gamma_j = \gamma;\ \boldsymbol{q}_i = \boldsymbol{q}_j = \boldsymbol{q}, \text{ for all } i, j; \tag{5.6}$$

$$p_k = \sum_s \gamma Z_{sk} q_s. \tag{5.7}$$

Proof. From the Modigliani–Miller theorem 4.2 we can construct a full set of Arrow–Debreu securities, in addition to the original spanning set, and all agents are indifferent to their introduction. Denoting the Arrow–Debreu prices by $\gamma q_s = p_s$, statements (5.6) and (5.7) follow by the Modigliani–Miller theorem. Eliminating the original spanning set of assets (the elimination is welfare-irrelevant), we are left with an Arrow–Debreu asset economy equilibrium. By the first fundamental theorem it is Pareto optimal.

The importance of this result is that in statements (5.6) and (5.7) the personalized Arrow–Debreu prices are equalized. Furthermore, from (5.7) we can deduce γ and q from market data. That is, given $K = S$ assets with rank $[\boldsymbol{Z}_1, \ldots, \boldsymbol{Z}_K] = S$, then $\boldsymbol{p} = \gamma \boldsymbol{q} \boldsymbol{Z}$, or

$$\gamma \boldsymbol{q} = \boldsymbol{p} \boldsymbol{Z}^{-1}. \tag{5.8}$$

Now by the Modigliani–Miller theorem we can construct a riskless asset $\boldsymbol{Z}_R = 1$ from the spanning set of assets, and deduce its equilibrium price $p_R = (1 + r)^{-1}$. By (5.5) we know that $\gamma = (1 + r)^{-1}$, so that (5.8) becomes:

$$\boldsymbol{q} = (1 + r)\boldsymbol{p}\boldsymbol{Z}^{-1}. \tag{5.9}$$

Condition (5.9) provides a method for deducing Arrow–Debreu prices from the $t = 0$ prices, and contingent returns matrix of the K assets. Indeed, it is a generalization of the two-state example in Chapter 4 where we analysed binomial option-pricing, and an alternative derivation of the Arrow–Debreu pricing result. There we obtained the result with induced preferences.

The general Theorem 5.2 can be illustrated with a familiar example.

Returning to the binomial option-pricing example of Chapter 4, recall:

$$p_{AD1} = (1 + r)^{-1}\left[\frac{(1 + r) - d}{u - d}\right]$$

$$p_{AD2} = (1 + r)^{-1}\left[\frac{u - (1 + r)}{u - d}\right].$$

Defining
$$q_1 \equiv \left[\frac{(1 + r) - d}{u - d}\right]$$

$$q_2 \equiv \left[\frac{u - (1 + r)}{u - d}\right].$$

We have
$$p_{AD1} = (1 + r)^{-1} q_1$$

$$p_{AD2} = (1 + r)^{-1} q_2$$

and
$$q_1 + q_2 = 1.$$

That is, q_1, q_2 are the martingale prices before discounting. We can provide a further example of deriving Arrow–Debreu prices, when a stock and a bond do not span the state space, but the introduction of a third asset will allow spanning.

Consider there to be three states of the world ($S = 3$). Let there be a stock, s, a riskless bond, b, and a call option, c, on the stock with an exercise price $K = p_s m$. Let the states be u (up), m (middle), and d (down). The matrix Z takes the form shown in Table 5.1.

TABLE 5.1

		Asset		
		s	*b*	*c*
State	*u*	$p_s \cdot u$	$1 + r$	$p_s u - K$
	m	$p_s \cdot m$	$1 + r$	0
	d	$p_s \cdot d$	$1 + r$	0

Clearly the three assets span the three-dimensional state space and the returns are linearly independent. Notice that the call option cannot be priced by arbitrage by taking a portfolio of the stock and the bond, but the call is required to span the asset-return space. We know from (5.9) that the Z matrix can be inverted, and by observing the current prices of the stock, p_s, bond (price equal to unity), and the call option, p_c, then we can solve for the Arrow–Debreu prices, q.

Given the Arrow–Debreu prices, then we can price any other security. For example, consider another call option on the stock with an exercise price $K = p_s \cdot d$. The price of this option, p_{c2}, will be given by:

$$p_{c2} = \sum_{s=1}^{3} \frac{Z_{c2}(s)}{1+r} q_s,$$

where $Z_{c2}(s) = \text{Max}\,[p_s \cdot s - K, 0]$, $s = u, m, d$.

This example is a special case of an argument employed by a number of authors (e.g. Banz and Miller, 1978). The most recent version of this idea is contained in Madan and Milne (1992), where the asset-return space is a Hilbert space that allows for infinite states, but exploits the linear pricing structure.

NON-DIFFERENTIABLE UTILITY

At the beginning of this chapter we observed that martingale pricing methods can be adapted to the case where

$U_i()$ is non-differentiable. This appears to be a minor issue, but recently there has been work on preferences under uncertainty, which are not differentiable (see Epstein and Wang, 1992, and Kelsey and Milne, 1992*b*). As we will show, the generalization is relatively easy, so that we can incorporate this recent work on preferences.

To begin, consider contingent consumption over two states, and preferences which, apart from non-differentiability, are neoclassical. At any consumption bundle x_i^* we can draw an indifference curve

$$\{\boldsymbol{x}_i \in \mathbb{R}_+^2 \mid U_i(\boldsymbol{x}_i) \geqslant U_i(\boldsymbol{x}_i^*)\}.$$

In Figure 5.1(*a*) we illustrate the differentiable case with a unique gradient $\nabla \boldsymbol{U}_i(\boldsymbol{x}_i^*)$;

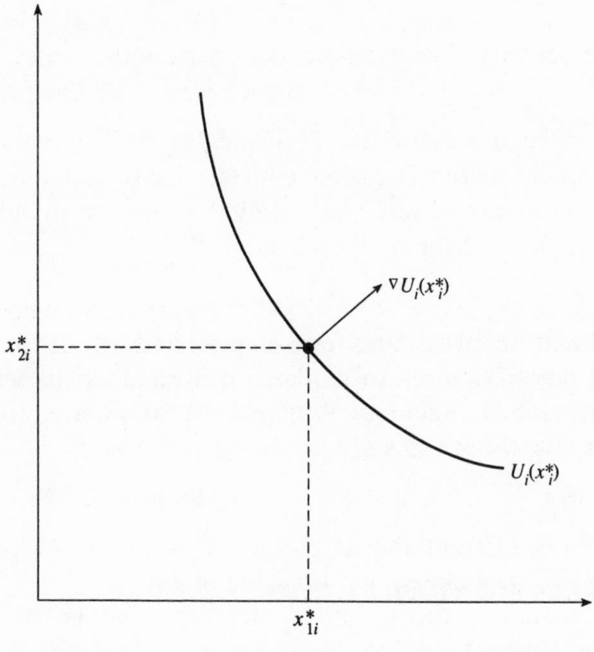

Fig. 5.1a

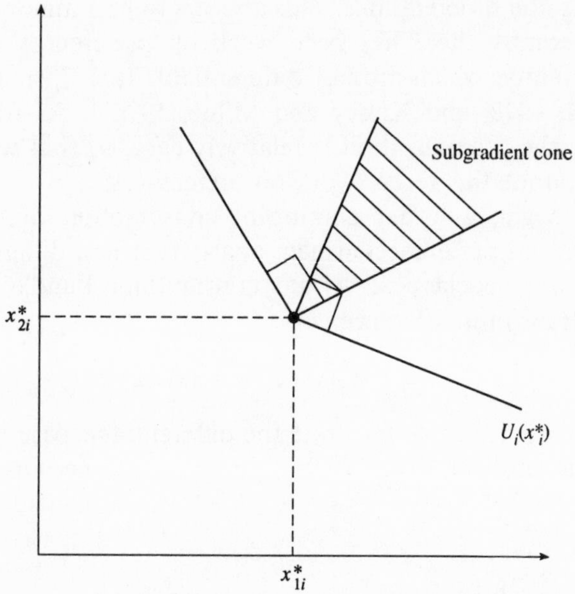

Fig. 5.1b

and in Figure 5.1(*b*) we illustrate the non-differentiable case where there is a closed, convex cone of subgradients.

Now we can modify our analysis to deal with subgradients. Because the preferred set at $\boldsymbol{x}_i^*$,

$$\mathscr{P}_i(\boldsymbol{x}_i^*) \equiv \{\boldsymbol{x}_i \in X_i \mid U_i(\boldsymbol{x}_i) \geqslant U_i(\boldsymbol{x}_i^*)\}$$

is closed, convex, and non-empty, and $\boldsymbol{x}_i^*$ is on the boundary of that set, we can use the Minkowski separating hyperplane theorem (see Varian, 1992 for a discussion) to show that there exists a

$$\boldsymbol{\pi}_i \in \mathbb{R}^{S+1} \text{ such that } \boldsymbol{\pi}_i \boldsymbol{x}_i \geqslant \boldsymbol{\pi}_i \boldsymbol{x}_i^* \text{ for all } \boldsymbol{x}_i \in \mathscr{P}_i(\boldsymbol{x}_i^*).$$

If $U_i()$ is differentiable at $\boldsymbol{x}_i^*$ then $\boldsymbol{\pi}_i$ is unique; otherwise there will be a closed, convex cone of $\boldsymbol{\pi}_i$'s.

In economic theory terms, the vector $\boldsymbol{\pi}_i$ is the consumer's (generalized) marginal rate of substitution. Or, we can think of π_i as the consumer's shadow prices over consumption bundles, using $\boldsymbol{x}_i^*$ as the reference consumption bundle.

We can write a generalization of (5.2) and (5.3), where

$$\nabla \tilde{\boldsymbol{U}}_i(\boldsymbol{x}_i^*) \text{ is a subgradient of } (\boldsymbol{x}_i^*).$$

The normalizations to γ_i and $\boldsymbol{q}_i$ can be applied to each subgradient vector in the usual way. Furthermore, Theorem 5.1 remains true: this is not surprising because Theorem 4.1 did not require differentiable utility.

If the assets span the state space, then Theorem 5.2 holds. Notice that all consumers will have the Arrow–Debreu prices lying in their optimal subgradient. This implies that arbitrage arguments on asset-pricing do not require differentiable utility—an observation we made in Chapter 4.

CONCLUSION

This chapter introduced martingale pricing methods and showed how they could be used to obtain arbitrage pricing methods. The next chapter exploits induced preference and martingale pricing arguments when spanning is not feasible.

6

Representative Consumers

An alternative route to asset-pricing can be obtained when spanning is not feasible. This subclass of models has evolved in parallel with the arbitrage models, and in many cases the same pricing formulae can be derived.

Consider a simple example of three states of the world and two securities.

$$\begin{array}{ccc} & \textit{Stock} & \textit{Bond} \\ \begin{array}{r} s=1 \\ 2 \\ 3 \end{array} & \begin{bmatrix} 3 \\ 2 \\ 1 \end{bmatrix} & \begin{bmatrix} 1 \\ 1 \\ 1 \end{bmatrix} \end{array}$$

Clearly these two security returns span a linear subspace of dimension 2 and do not span the whole of $\mathbb{R}^3$. Therefore if a security is introduced that is not spanned by the stock and the bond, it cannot be priced by arbitrage. Furthermore, its introduction will not be welfare-neutral. The reason is straightforward: the new asset will increase the opportunities for contingent trades perturbing the equilibrium asset, and contingent commodity allocations, and the asset and personalized contingent prices.

Nevertheless, there are cases where the introduction of the new asset will be welfare-neutral and the asset can be priced by the (undisturbed) contingent prices.

IDENTICAL CONSUMERS

Assume that each of the I consumers has identical preferences and endowments. It is obvious that we can analyse the case of this economy with a single consumer, treating the replicas in an identical fashion. In what follows we will merely assume $I = 1$.

Consider the optimum problem for the contingent commodity problem:

$$\text{Max } U_1(x_{01}, x_{11}, \ldots, x_{S1}).$$

$$s.t. \quad x_{01} = \bar{x}_{01} + \sum_j y_{0j}$$

$$x_{s1} = \sum_j y_{sj}, \quad s = 1, \ldots, S.$$

$$(y_{0j}, y_{1j}, \ldots, y_{sj}) \in Y_j, \quad j = 1, \ldots, J.$$

By the second fundamental theorem, we know that this trivial Pareto optimum can be supported by contingent prices $(p_0, p_1, \ldots, p_s)$ such that there is competitive equilibrium at the optimum allocation. By construction:

$$x^*_{01} = \bar{x}_{01} + \sum_j y^*_{0j} \equiv \bar{x}_0$$

$$x^*_{s1} = \sum_j y^*_{sj} \equiv \bar{x}_s, \quad s = 1, \ldots, S.$$

Now introduce assets into this economy. Assume that the allocations $[(x^*_{s1}), (y^*_{sj})]$ lie in the span of $[\boldsymbol{Z}_1, \ldots, \boldsymbol{Z}_k]$. Notice that there is no reason why the asset returns should span the full state space in general. In particular, if the economy is an exchange economy with no production, asset returns merely require that there exists $(\bar{a}_k)$ such that

$$x^*_{s1} = \sum_k Z_{sk}\bar{a}_k.$$

We can introduce the asset markets without altering the consumer's contingent allocation (or welfare) so long as asset-prices are given by

$$p_k = \sum_{s=1}^{S} p_s Z_{sk} = \sum_{s=1}^{S} \gamma_1 Z_{sk} q_{s1}.$$

Furthermore, we know from Chapter 5, that (γ_1, q_{s1}) are derived from the gradient of $U_1()$ evaluated at $(\bar{x}_0, \bar{x}_1, \ldots, \bar{x}_s)$.

Therefore, if we can evaluate this gradient at the equilibrium aggregate consumption, then we have a method for pricing assets. Notice that we can price any asset if we make the assumption that any additional asset added is in zero net supply. Trivially

$$\bar{x}_s = x_s^* = \sum_{k=1}^{K} Z_{sk}\bar{a}_k + Z_{sK+1} \cdot \bar{a}_{K+1}$$

when $$\bar{a}_{K+1} = 0.$$

Although this model is ridiculously simple, it has been used extensively to provide pricing for assets that cannot be reproduced by arbitrage. (For example, Rubinstein, 1976; Brennan, 1979; Stapleton and Subrahmanyan, 1984; Madan and Milne, 1992.)

In fact, we can generalize this result a little to allow for changes in proportional endowments by assuming that consumers have affine homothetic preferences, such that apart from the affine component, they are identical. The intuition is straightforward. Apart from an endowment scale effect, the consumers are identical, so that a representative consumer can be constructed, and the allocation is Pareto optimal.

For expository ease we will prove the homothetic case first for an exchange economy, treating the affine homothetic case as a simple corollary.

THEOREM 6.1. *Given an asset exchange economy, assume that each consumer has:*

(i) *Neoclassical preferences* $U_i() = \phi_i(\tilde{U}())$, *where* ϕ_i *is a differentiable, strictly increasing function; and* $\tilde{U}()$ *is homogeneous of degree 1; then the equilibrium contingent allocation is Pareto optimal and* $\gamma_i q_{si} = p_s$ *for all i and s.*

Proof. Consider any consumer's induced problem. Because $U_i()$ is homothetic, then it is easy to prove that the induced utility function $V_i(x_{0i}, \boldsymbol{a}_i)$ is homothetic. From standard consumer theory, we know that the consumer demands can be written as

$$\alpha_k(p_0^*, \ldots, p_K^*) \cdot W_{0i} \quad \text{for} \quad k = 0, 1, \ldots, K.$$

Notice that $\alpha_k()$ is independent of i because $\tilde{U}$ is common for all consumers. Thus

$$x_{si}^* = \sum_k Z_{sk}\alpha_k(p_0^*, \ldots, p_K^*) \cdot W_{0i},$$

for all $\qquad s = 0, 1, \ldots, 1; \quad \text{or} \quad x_{si}^* = x_s^*()\, W_{0i}.$

Taking the gradient of $\tilde{U}(\boldsymbol{x}^*)$ we obtain a unique vector $(\boldsymbol{p}_0, \boldsymbol{p}_1, \ldots, \boldsymbol{p}_s) \equiv \boldsymbol{p}$ of Arrow–Debreu prices. Consider the new consumer problem: Max $U_i(\boldsymbol{x}_i)$, subject to $\boldsymbol{p}^*\boldsymbol{x}_i \leqslant \boldsymbol{p}\boldsymbol{x}_i^*$, for each consumer. By the first fundamental theorem, $[(\boldsymbol{x}_i^*)]$ is a Pareto optimal allocation. By the standard normalization we have $\gamma_i q_{si} = p_s$ and $\gamma_i = \gamma$, $q_{si} = q_s$, for all i.

Note that the case of identical consumers (with non-homothetic preferences) is really a degenerate case, where no differences in wealth are allowed.

Now we can allow for affine translations of utility to obtain a generalization of the theorem.

Corollary 6.1. Given the hypotheses of the theorem, let the utility function be

$$U_i(\boldsymbol{x}_i) = \phi(\tilde{U}(\bar{\boldsymbol{x}}_i + \boldsymbol{x}_i))$$

where there exists β_{ki} such that

$$\bar{x}_{si} = \sum_k Z_{sk}\beta_{ki},$$

then the conclusions of the theorem follow.

Proof. By treating the β_i as a *de facto* endowment of assets for consumer i, let

$$\alpha_k() \equiv \beta_{ki} + \alpha_{ki}()$$

where α_{ki} is the net trade of assets. The theorem now applies trivially.

As we observed before, we can add assets in zero net supply to this economy in a welfare-neutral fashion without disturbing the Arrow–Debreu (martingale) prices. Formally, we have the following obvious result:

Corollary 6.2. Given a representative consumer then any asset can be priced as

$$p_k = \sum_s \gamma Z_{sk} q_s.$$

Proof. Obvious implication of Theorem 6.1.

VON NEUMANN–MORGENSTERN PREFERENCES AND AGGREGATION

We observed in Chapter 2 that in an Arrow–Debreu economy, with von Neumann–Morgenstern preferences and affine homothetic preferences, then the utility function must be of the form:

$$u_i(x_s) = \begin{cases} \delta(x_s + \alpha_i)^c & 0 < c < 1 \\ \lambda \ln(\delta x_s + \alpha_i), & \\ \lambda \exp(\delta x_s), & \lambda < 0; \delta < 0. \end{cases}$$

Because this utility function is affine homothetic with Arrow–Debreu securities, then more general securities may reduce the applicability of this class. As it turns out, the class is barely reduced; and if we include a riskless asset, the class is not reduced at all. (See Cass–Stiglitz, 1970; Milne, 1979, Theorem 5.)

Therefore, if we assume that all consumers have utility functions in this class, and the parameters are all chosen so that there is an aggregate consumer, we will obtain a unique martingale pricing formula.

The Aggregate Consumer and Option Pricing

Rubinstein (1976) considers the case where all consumers have utility functions of the form:

$$u_0(x_0) + u_1(x_s) = \frac{1}{1-B} x_0^{1-B} + \rho \frac{1}{1-B} x_s^{1-B}.$$

Now recall our pricing equation:

$$p_k = \sum_s Z_{sk} \gamma_i q_{si}.$$

But, we know that with von Neumann–Morgenstern preferences, intertemporal additive separability, and the existence of a riskless asset,

$$q_{si} = u_i'(x_{si}^*)\pi_s(\lambda \cdot \gamma)^{-1};$$

$$\lambda = u_0'(x_{0i}^*), \quad \text{assuming } p_0 = 1;$$

and

$$\gamma = (1+r)^{-1}.$$

Thus

$$q_{si} = \frac{u_i'(x_{si}^*)}{u_0'(x_0^*)} \pi_s(1+r)$$

and

$$p_k = \sum_s (1+r)^{-1} Z_{sk} \left[\frac{u_i'(x_{si}^*)}{u_0'(x_{0i}^*)} \pi_s(1+r) \right]$$

$$= \sum_s Z_{sk} \left[\frac{u_i'(x_{si}^*)}{u_0'(x_0^*)} \pi_s \right]$$

$$= \sum_s \left[Z_{sk} \frac{u_i'(x_{si}^*)}{u_0'(x_0^*)} \right] \pi_s$$

$$= E_\pi \left[Z_{sk} \frac{u_i'(x_{si}^*)}{u_0'(x_{0i}^*)} \right].$$

Because of aggregation, we obtain:

$$p_k = E_\pi\left[Z_{sk}\frac{u_i'(\bar{x}_s)}{u_i'(\bar{x}_0)}\right]$$

$$= \rho E_\pi\left[Z_{sk}\left(\frac{\bar{x}_0}{\bar{x}_s}\right)^B\right].$$

Now Rubinstein wishes to obtain a formula for pricing call options, i.e. $Z_{sk} = \text{Max}\,[0, p(s) - K]$, where $p_s(S)$ is the price of a share in state s, p_c is the price of the call at $t = 0$, and K is the exercise price. This gives us

$$p_c = \rho E_\pi\left[\text{Max}\,[0, p_s(s) - K]\left(\frac{\bar{x}_0}{\bar{x}_s}\right)^B\right].$$

Unfortunately, this still depends upon the true probability measure which is yet unspecified. Rubinstein assumes that $p(s)$ and $\bar{x}_s$ are bivariate lognormally distributed, i.e. $\ln(p)$ and $\ln\bar{x}$ are bivariate normally distributed. Notice that this specification requires an infinite set of states, but our finite arguments can be extended in a straightforward fashion by replacing sums with integrals. With some tedious calculations (see Rubinstein, 1976; Huang and Litzenberger, 1988: 163–6) it can be shown that:

$$p_c = pN(Z + \sigma_S) - (1 + r)^{-1}KN(Z), \tag{5.1}$$

where

$$N(Z) = \frac{1}{\surd(2\pi)}\int_{-\infty}^{Z}\exp(-u^2/2)\,du,$$

is the normal distribution function; σ_S is the variance of the share price; and

$$Z \equiv \frac{\ln(p/K) + \ln(1 + r)}{\sigma_S} - \frac{1}{2}\sigma_S.$$

Now equation (5.1) is the celebrated Black–Scholes (1973) option-pricing equation. Whereas Black–Scholes derived the equation using continuous-time Brownian motion for the stock price and arbitrage arguments, Rubinstein was able to derive the same formula, using discrete time and specific restrictions on a representative consumer.

Notice that the Rubinstein derivation does not assume spanning, or arbitrage, but relies merely on aggregation and the judicious choice of utility and probability distributions. Although the derivation focuses on the pricing of a call option, it relies on the construction of an Arrow–Debreu measure over the future share price (the 'state of the world'). Therefore, in principle, any contingent claim can be priced.

The Aggregate Consumer and General Contingent Claims

Stapleton and Subrahmanyam (1984) extended the models of Rubinstein and Brennan (1979) by using the representative agent model to price complex contingent claims that go beyond the simple call option. The reader should observe that the following theorem is a numerically tractable example of our more general Theorem 6.1 and its two corollaries.

THEOREM 6.2. *(Stapleton and Subrahmanyam). Given a representative consumer with* $u(x) = \exp(\delta x)$, *and that the finite set of underlying stochastic variables and wealth are multivariate normally distributed, then any complex asset price* $p_k = (1 + r)^{-1} E(Z_k)$, *where the Arrow–Debreu prices are derived as functions of the means and covariances of the underlying distribution.*

Proof. For a proof and examples, see Stapleton and Subrahmanyam (1984).

BEYOND VON NEUMANN–MORGENSTERN REPRESENTATIVE AGENTS

Recently there has been interest in preference structures that go beyond von Neumann–Morgenstern utility. Epstein and Zinn (1989, 1991) analyse preferences that are more flexible than von Neumann–Morgenstern and allow for different specifications of risk-aversion and intertemporal rates of substitution. (The additively separable von Neumann–Morgenstern model of Rubinstein, and Stapleton and Subrahmanyam could not allow such a distinction.) Although strictly speaking, Epstein and Zinn have a multi-period model, the intuition of their result is captured by our two-date homothetic representative consumer: asset prices are derived as the gradient of their recursive utility at the endowment point.

An alternative approach has been to avoid choice under risk with objective probabilities, and consider variants of models under uncertainty. Our framework with preferences over contingent consumption is flexible enough to incorporate either specification. Consider the recent work of Epstein and Wang (1992). They draw upon work by Gilboa and Schmeidler (1989), specifying a utility function which is a Choquet integral. In short, this is a utility function with 'probabilities' that do not add up to one, and reflect uncertainty aversion. (We will not discuss the details here as they would require an extended treatment.) But for our purposes, we observe that with a representative consumer with homothetic preferences of this form, the utility function will not be differentiable at the endowment. It follows directly from our discussion of non-differentiable preferences in Chapter 5, that we can extend Theorem 5.1 and its corollaries to the non-differentiable case and obtain non-unique supporting Arrow–Debreu prices. This is the essence of Epstein–Wang's indeterminancy of asset-pricing.

APPROXIMATING MARGINAL UTILITY OF A REPRESENTATIVE AGENT

Instead of exploring different functional forms of utility for the representative agent, we can assume the existence of a general homothetic preference relation and its associated supporting Arrow–Debreu prices. Now, decompose the $\boldsymbol{q}$ vector as a linear combination of a few 'factors', i.e.

$$\sum_f \alpha_f \boldsymbol{q}_f = \boldsymbol{q}.$$

With a finite state space this is relatively trivial, but in infinite dimensional spaces the idea of factor decomposition is more complex.

Madan and Milne (1992) explore this idea with Hilbert space techniques, using Hermite polynomials as an example. One interpretation of this approach is to assume the existence of a representative consumer so that the addition of assets in zero net supply will be welfare-neutral. Using a subset of the existing assets to estimate the coefficients $\{\alpha_f\}$, and identify the factors $\boldsymbol{q}_f$, one can price any new assets as a linear function of a few Arrow–Debreu factors.

CONCLUSION

In this chapter we have set out the basic tools of the representative agent model for pricing assets. As we showed, the central idea is straightforward, but more complex in application. It is important in these models not to lose sight of the central simple story that drives the pricing result.

7

Diversification and Asset-Pricing

So far, we have concentrated on two major methods for asset-pricing: arbitrage and consumer aggregation. In both discussions we have not mentioned one of the important traditional topics in finance theory—diversification. In this chapter, we will explore the idea of portfolio diversification and its implications for asset-pricing. The analysis will be at a fairly abstract level; but it will become apparent that traditional arguments can be included as special cases of the more general framework. The abstract discussion focuses on the essential issues without the distracting clutter of more restrictive assumptions that hide the simple logic that drives the central results. (For a more detailed discussion, see Milne, 1988.)

ARBITRAGE AND DIVERSIFICATION

Consider a consumer with induced preferences over assets and a budget constraint. Assume that the asset returns $[\boldsymbol{Z}_1, \ldots, \boldsymbol{Z}_K]$ are linearly independent. (Although the reader can think of these returns to be in $\mathbb{R}^S$, the argument is general and can be applied to more general vector spaces.) Now we can create portfolios, priced by arbitrage, to create another set of assets called 'factors'. Factor returns will be constructed by:

$$\boldsymbol{F}_f = \sum_k \alpha_{kf} \boldsymbol{Z}_k, \quad f = 1, \ldots, \mathcal{F}.$$

By arbitrage pricing, factor prices are related to the underlying asset-prices by

$$p_f = \sum_k \alpha_{kf} p_k.$$

Now we can relate factor and underlying asset returns by the simple construction of 'deviations' or idiosyncratic returns $\boldsymbol{\epsilon}_k$, such that

$$\boldsymbol{\epsilon}_k \equiv \boldsymbol{Z}_k - \sum_f \beta_{fk} \boldsymbol{F}_f;$$

or

$$\boldsymbol{Z}_k = \sum_f \beta_{fk} \boldsymbol{F}_f + \boldsymbol{\epsilon}_k. \tag{7.1}$$

Again, by arbitrage pricing we can price the asset k in terms of the factor prices and the deviation prices, i.e.

$$p_k = \sum_f \beta_{fk} p_f + p_{\varepsilon_k}. \tag{7.2}$$

So far we have done nothing other than make repeated applications of the generalized Modiglian–Miller theorem.

Now to introduce the idea of diversification across assets, let us introduce some additional assumptions on the structure of the $\boldsymbol{\epsilon}_k$'s; and consumer attitudes to portfolios that include 'undiversified' collections of the $\boldsymbol{\epsilon}$'s.

Let us assume that there are portfolios which are diversified, that is:

A.1. There exists portfolios $\{\alpha_k^f\}$ such that $\sum_k \boldsymbol{\epsilon}_k \alpha_k^f = 0$ and that $\boldsymbol{B}\alpha^f \neq 0$ for $f = 1, \ldots, \mathcal{F}$, where $\boldsymbol{B} = [\beta_{kf}]$.

The idea here is that consumers are able to create portfolios which are composed solely of the factors. Indeed, they are able to create portfolios that are *any* linear combination of the factors $1, \ldots, \mathcal{F}$.

The second assumption introduces the idea that the consumer dislikes undiversified portfolios. Or, more precisely, given two portfolios with the same factor returns, the consumer will desire the portfolio which 'diversifies away' the $\boldsymbol{\epsilon}_k$ terms.

Before we do that, it will be convenient to create an economy with returns $[\boldsymbol{Z}_1, \ldots, \boldsymbol{Z}_K; \boldsymbol{F}_1, \ldots, \boldsymbol{F}_{\mathcal{F}}; \boldsymbol{\epsilon}_1, \ldots, \boldsymbol{\epsilon}_K]$ and prices defined by arbitrage. Now we can consider portfolios that are 'factor equivalent', but differ in the addition of nontrivial $\boldsymbol{\epsilon}_k$ 'risk'.

A.2. For any consumer, and any $\{\alpha_f^F\}$, given non-trivial $\{\alpha_k^\varepsilon\}$ such that

$$\sum_k \alpha_k^\varepsilon \boldsymbol{\epsilon}_k \neq 0,$$

then $$V_i\left(x_{0i}; \left(\sum_k \alpha_k^\varepsilon \boldsymbol{\epsilon}_k + \sum_f \alpha_f^F \boldsymbol{F}_f\right)\right) < V_i\left(x_{0i}; \left(\sum_f \alpha_f^F \boldsymbol{F}_f\right)\right).$$

To derive some pricing results we will introduce one final assumption:

A.3. $V_i()$ is differentiable.

We are now in a position to prove the following theorem.

THEOREM 7.1. *Given a consumer that satisfies A.2 and A.3; and returns satisfy A.1, and if the consumer holds a diversified portfolio at the optimum, then*

$$p^*_{\varepsilon_k} = 0, \textit{ for all } k; \quad \textit{and } p^*_k = \sum_f \beta_{kf} p^*_f.$$

Proof. Given a diversified portfolio $\{a_{fi}^F\}$, then the consumer will reduce utility by holding an undiversified $\{a_{ki}^\varepsilon\}$. Thus the gradient of $V_i()$ with respect to a_{ki}^ε at the optimum is zero, i.e.

$$\frac{\partial V_i\left(x_{0i}^\alpha; \left(\sum_k \alpha_{ki}^\varepsilon \boldsymbol{\epsilon}_k + \sum_f a_{fi}^F \boldsymbol{F}_f\right)\right)}{\partial a_{ki}^\varepsilon} = 0, \text{ for all } k.$$

But at the consumer's optimum $\dfrac{\partial V_i()}{\partial a_{ki}^\varepsilon} = \lambda_i p_{\varepsilon_k}$, with $\lambda_i > 0$; which implies

$p_{\varepsilon_k} = 0$, for all k. Because $p_k = \sum_f \beta_{hf} p_f + p_{\varepsilon_k}$, then $p_k = \sum_f \beta_{kf} p_f$.

Note. That this result is a generalization of Chen and Ingersoll (1983).

Although this result is interesting in itself, it does not explain why a consumer will hold a diversified portfolio. With one more assumption we can show that every consumer will hold a diversified portfolio.

A.4. Given an asset exchange economy, then the aggregate endowment of assets is well diversified, i.e.

$$\sum_i \sum_k \varepsilon_k \bar{a}_{ki} = 0.$$

With this assumption in hand, we can show that all consumers will choose well-diversified portfolios.

THEOREM 7.2. *Given A.1, A.2, and A.4 then in a competitive equilibrium, all consumers will hold fully diversified portfolios.*

Proof. We know that an equilibrium is a (constrained) Pareto optimum. Assume the equilibrium has consumers holding non-diversified portfolios. Then we can always find a set of consumers who can exchange portfolios of idiosyncratic assets and improve their welfare. This is feasible given that the aggregate endowment is fully diversifiable.

Now given Theorems 7.1 and 7.2, we obtain the general arbitrage-pricing theorem (APT).

THEOREM 7.3. *Given consumers who satisfy A.2 and A.3 and assets that satisfy A.1 and A.4, then asset prices will satisfy*

$$p_k = \sum_f \beta_{fk} p_f.$$

Proof. Trivial application of Theorem 7.1 and Theorem 7.2.

With this general structure in place, we can show how it can be used as a flexible tool of analysis. As an illustration we will introduce the traditional mean-variance analysis of portfolio theory and show how it can be fitted into our general framework.

Mean-Variance Analysis and CAPM

Consider a consumer who faces $K + 1$ assets. The first asset is riskless, and the remainder are multivariate normally distributed. Given that the consumer has von Neumann–Morgenstern preferences over $t = 1$ consumption (we ignore $t = 0$ consumption), we can write:

$$V_i(\boldsymbol{a}_i) = \int \ldots \int u_i\left(\sum_{k=1} a_{ki}Z_k + 1 \cdot a_{0i}\right) f(Z_1, \ldots, Z_K)dZ_1, \ldots, dZ_K,$$

where $f()$ is the multivariate normal density function, with a K vector of means and a covariance matrix of dimension K.

The normal distribution has the convenient property that linear combinations of multivariate normally distributed random variables are normally distributed.

Furthermore we can construct a market portfolio of the risky assets such that

$$Z_m \equiv \sum_{k=1}^{K} Z_k \bar{a}_k, \quad \text{where} \quad \bar{a}_k = \sum_i \bar{a}_{ki}.$$

By considering the market portfolio m as one factor, and the riskless asset as another factor, we can write

$$\varepsilon_k \equiv Z_k - \beta_{k0} \cdot 1 - \beta_{km} F_m,$$

where

$$\beta_{km} = \text{cov}(Z_k, Z_m)/\text{var}(Z_m); \quad \beta_{k0} = E(Z_k); \quad \text{and} \quad F_m \equiv Z_m - E(Z_m).$$

In other words, every asset return Z_k can be written as a linear combination of two normally distributed random variables F_m and ε_k, and the riskless asset. In addition, the random variables have been constructed so that $E(\varepsilon_j | F_m) = 0$. It is not difficult to check that these returns have been constructed to satisfy A.1 and that

$$\sum_k \varepsilon_k \bar{a}_k = 0 \ \text{(i.e. A.4)}.$$

With some extra effort you can show that the induced preferences satisfy A.2 and 3. Thus we deduce from Theorem 7.2 that all consumers will hold diversified portfolios. That is, they will hold only combinations of the riskless asset and the 'market' portfolio, i.e. the portfolio of all risky assets. This result is known as the two fund separation theorem for mean-variance portfolios.

To obtain our asset-pricing result, notice that

$$Z_k = \beta_{k0} \cdot 1 + \beta_{km} F_m + \varepsilon_k = E(Z_k) + \beta_{km} F_m + \varepsilon_k.$$

Thus by Theorem 7.3, we deduce that

$$p_k = E(Z_k) p_0 + \beta_{km} p_{Fm} + p_{\varepsilon_k},$$

where $p_{\varepsilon_k} = 0$ and p_{Fm} is the price of the market portfolio. Recalling $F_m \equiv Z_m - E(Z_m)$, and that the price of m is p_m, then

$$p_{Fm} = p_m - E(Z_m) p_0.$$

By definition, let $r = (p_0)^{-1} - 1$. Thus

$$p_k = (1 + r)^{-1} [E(Z_k) + [p_m(1 + r) - E(Z_m)]\beta_{km}]. \quad (7.3)$$

If we define the rates of return,

$$R_k = \frac{Z_k - p_k}{p_k}$$

then it is possible to show that (7.3) becomes:

$$E(R_k) = R_0 + [E(R_m) - R_0]\beta_{km}. \quad (7.4)$$

This is the celebrated CAPM formula.

CONNOR'S (1984) APT

The CAPM is perhaps the most famous, and restrictive of the APT family of models: it assumes von Neumann–Morgenstern preferences and multivariate normally distributed returns for the risky assets. In the 1970s Ross (1976) extended the theory by assuming von Neumann–Morgenstern preferences, but a factor structure on returns, such that the idiosyncratic risks could be diversified away. Subsequently, a number of authors attempted to place this argument on a rigorous and more general basis. Connor (1984) assumed differentiable von Neumann–Morgenstern preferences and a factor structure of returns. His theory exploited the properties of general equilibrium to show a special case of our general theorems above. In addition, he allowed for a countable number of assets, so that diversification could be achieved by a law of large numbers, rather than finite linear dependence.

APT THEOREMS WITHOUT VON NEUMANN–MORGENSTERN PREFERENCES

In our general proofs (Theorems 7.1–7.3) we did not rely upon von Neumann–Morgenstern preferences, but upon properties of induced preferences over assets. In Kelsey and Milne (1992*b*) the general framework is extended to an infinity of assets *and* introduces non-expected utility preferences. With a careful specification of the notion of risk-aversion, and the assumption of a factor structure of returns, they were able to show that the induced preferences will inherit the properties assumed above. Therefore, Kelsey–Milne have extended the APT to classes of non-expected utility theory. The reader should note that pure arbitrage results are robust to such generalizations; the complexities are introduced when we try to characterize risk or uncertainty avoidance.

APPROXIMATE APT

The reader should recall (7.2) where an application of the Modigliani–Miller theorem to the factor structure gave us an exact pricing equation with p_{ε_k} not necessarily zero. One can consider this equation and provide conditions under which p_{ε_k} is small, but not necessarily zero. A simple example of this argument would be where the economy has a representative consumer and A.4 does not hold, i.e. the endowment of the consumer is not diversified given the assumed factor structure of returns. (For a more detailed discussion of this argument and references to related literature, see Milne, 1988.)

CONCLUSION

In this chapter we have shown that arbitrage pricing arguments can be extended to allow for diversifiable risks. In equilibrium, these risks will be fully diversifiable and have zero price. Thus every asset can be priced exactly (or approximately) as a linear combination of a relatively small number of common factors.

8

Multiperiod Asset-Pricing: Complete Markets

So far, we have restricted attention to two-date models. Although this is instructive for introducing basic ideas of arbitrage, aggregation, and diversification, we require a multiperiod framework to capture a range of intertemporal problems. For example, we would like to investigate the term structure of interest rates, complicated multiperiod derivative securities, the dynamics of stock prices, and dynamic hedging strategies. It will turn out that our two-period analysis has laid an important foundation for this analysis. By choosing an appropriate dynamic framework, we can generalize our two-date results, and obtain obvious sophisticated reinterpretations of familiar results.

MULTIPERIOD UNCERTAINTY

Recall that we introduced uncertainty by defining contingent consumption, production, and asset returns on a simple tree. This tree structure can be extended to include many dates and states (or events) (Figure 8.1).

The events e_t are partial histories of the world up to time t. In our example, the tree has {12, 22} succeeding event 11, but the successor to 21 is only 32. In the first case, any agent at 11 will not know which event {12, 21} will occur, but knows that 23 is impossible. Conversely, if the agent is

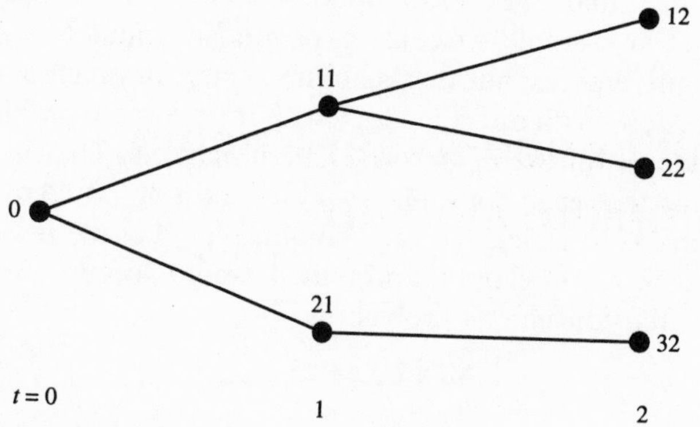

Fig. 8.1

at 12, then he/she knows with certainty that 32 will occur with certainty, but that {12, 21} is impossible. Formally, we can define the events $\{e_t\}$ as a partially ordered tree with a unique 'root' e_0.

Now using the same trick as in the two-date model, we can define contingent commodities, trades, returns, etc., according to which node of the tree we are considering. In this formal sense, all we are doing is enlarging the dimension of the commodity space to $E + 1$,

where $E = \sum_{t=1}^{T} \sum_{e=1}^{E_t} e_t$, and E_t is the number of events at t.

THE CONSUMER

Consider a consumer who has a consumption set

$$X_i = \mathbb{R}_+^{E+1},$$

and a utility function $U_i : X_i \to \mathbb{R}$. We will assume that $U_i()$ is continuous, quasi-concave, strictly increasing, and differentiable.

Notice that these assumptions include some special cases. For example, we could have von Neumann–Morgenstern preferences; but this is not necessary for much of our discussion. With direct analogy with the two-date problem, consider a full set of Arrow–Debreu markets. That is, we assume that each consumer can buy and sell, on competitive markets, claims for each contingency. Let the price at $t = 0$, for a unit claim if and only if event e_t occurs, be p_{e_t}. Thus, the consumer's problem is:

$$\left[\begin{array}{l} \underset{\{\boldsymbol{x}_i \in X_i\}}{\text{Max}}\ U_i(\boldsymbol{x}_i) \\ \boldsymbol{p}\boldsymbol{x}_i \leqslant \boldsymbol{p}\bar{\boldsymbol{x}}_i + \sum_j \theta_{ij}\boldsymbol{p}\boldsymbol{y}_j, \end{array}\right. \tag{8.1}$$

where $\bar{\boldsymbol{x}}_i \in \mathbb{R}^{E+1}$ is the consumer's endowment; and $\boldsymbol{y}_j \in \mathbb{R}^{E+1}$ is firm j's production vector.

THE FIRM

By direct analogy with the two-date problem we define the firm's production set

$$Y_j \subset \mathbb{R}^{E+1}.$$

Often we will characterize the firm's production technology by an implicit production function $F_j(\boldsymbol{y}_j) = 0$. Notice that positive components of $\boldsymbol{y}_j$ will be considered outputs, and negative components inputs.

The firm's problem can be written as:

$$\underset{\boldsymbol{y}_j \in Y_j}{\text{Max}}\ \boldsymbol{p}\boldsymbol{y}_j. \tag{8.2}$$

Putting this all together, we have:

DEFINITION 8.1. *A competitive equilibrium in a multiperiod Arrow–Debreu economy is a price vector* $p^* \in \mathbb{R}^{E+1}$, *and an allocation* $[(\boldsymbol{x}_i^*), (\boldsymbol{y}_j^*)]$ *such that:*

(i) x_i^* *is a solution to the consumer's problem for all i;*
(ii) y_j^* *is a solution to the producer's problem for all j;*
(iii) $\sum_j x_i^* = \sum_i \bar{x}_i + \sum_j y_j^*$.

In general we can apply standard arguments to the existence and optimality of the equilibrium. After all, we have merely expanded the dimension of the commodity space without altering any of the key assumptions.

SPECIAL CASES

1. A Single-Consumer Model: Certainty

Consider a simple economy with a single consumer and certainty, so that the commodity space is $\mathbb{R}^{T+1}$. We can exploit the second fundamental theorem of welfare economics to characterize the equilibrium of this economy. First, consider a Pareto optimum:

$$\left[\begin{array}{l} \max\limits_{x \in X} U(\boldsymbol{x}) \\ s.t.\ \boldsymbol{x} = \bar{\boldsymbol{x}} + \boldsymbol{y}; \\ \quad \boldsymbol{y} \in Y. \end{array}\right. \tag{8.3}$$

Notice that we have lumped together all the production activities into one 'firm'.

With standard assumptions on the consumption and production sets we can show that the set of feasible allocations

$$\{(\boldsymbol{x}, \boldsymbol{y}) \in \mathbb{R}^{2(T+1)} \mid \boldsymbol{x} \in X, \boldsymbol{y} \in Y; \boldsymbol{x} = \bar{\boldsymbol{x}} + \boldsymbol{y}\}$$

is closed and bounded. Given a continuous utility function then, by the Weierstrass theorem, an optimum exists. (This is just a special case of the more general existence theorem for the existence of Pareto optima.)

Now, if X, Y are both convex, and $U()$ is continuous, increasing, and quasi-concave, then we can apply the second fundamental theorem of welfare economics to show that we can support the optimum $(\boldsymbol{x}^*, \boldsymbol{y}^*)$ with competitive prices: $\boldsymbol{p} \gg 0$: i.e.:

$$\begin{bmatrix} \text{Max } U(\boldsymbol{x}) \\ \boldsymbol{px} = \boldsymbol{p\bar{x}} + \boldsymbol{py} \end{bmatrix} \tag{8.4}$$

$$\begin{bmatrix} \text{Max } \boldsymbol{py} \\ \boldsymbol{y} \in Y. \end{bmatrix} \tag{8.5}$$

For example, consider the consumer's problem when we assume $U()$ is differentiable and additively separable over time:

$$\text{Max} \sum_{t=0}^{T} \delta^t u(x_t)$$

$$\text{s.t.} \sum_{t=0}^{T} p_t x_t = \sum_{t=0}^{T} p_t \bar{x}_t + \sum_{t=0}^{T} p_t y_t,$$

where $0 < \delta < 1$, and $u'() > 0$, $u''() < 0$.
From the first-order conditions for an interior maximum we have:

$$\delta u'(x_t^*) = \lambda p_t.$$

If we postulated a particular form for the subutility function (ln() or exp() say), numerical values for the subjective discount factor $\delta \in (0, 1)$ and 'aggregate consumption' $\{x_t^*\}$, then we can solve numerically for the relative prices. Of course, this is very restrictive.

But what are the relative prices? The price p_t is the price at $t = 0$ for the delivery of a unit of the commodity at time t. How is this sequence of prices related to interest rates? We can derive interest rates via the following definitions:

$$\textit{Short rates} \quad \frac{p_{t+1}}{p_t} \equiv (1 + r_{t,t+1})^{-1}$$

$$\textit{Long rates} \quad \frac{p_{t+\tau}}{p_t} \equiv (1 + r_{t,\,t+\tau})^{-\tau}.$$

By definition we have that

$$\frac{p_{t+\tau}}{p_t} = \frac{p_{t+\tau}}{p_{t+\tau-1}} \cdot \frac{p_{t+\tau-1}}{p_{t+\tau-2}} \cdots \frac{p_{t+1}}{p_t},$$

or $(1 + r_{t,\,t+\tau})^{-\tau} = (1 + r_{t+\tau-1,\,t+\tau})^{-1} \ldots (1 + r_{t,\,t+1})^{-1}$. (8.6)

This simple relation connects the long rate for any interval to the product of the short rates for the same interval. As we shall see later, this result can be obtained as an arbitrage result from an asset economy trading long and short bonds.

An important question is the determination of the short- and long-term interest rates. Because these rates are simply derived from present value prices $\{p_t\}$, then their determination relies on the properties of the preferences and endowment of the consumer and the production set. It is easy to construct examples where interest rates vary in all sorts of ways over time, so that the term structure rises, falls, or oscillates.

2. A SINGLE CONSUMER MODEL: UNCERTAINTY

A similar analysis can be carried out when the previous model is expanded to incorporate uncertainty. For simplicity, we will dispense with production and concentrate on the consumer's problem, and the interpretation of the first-order conditions for an optimum.

The problem now looks trivial:

$$\max_{\boldsymbol{x} = \bar{\boldsymbol{x}}} U(\boldsymbol{x}).$$

The price vector is proportional to the gradient of the consumer's utility function calculated at $\bar{\boldsymbol{x}}$.

$$\nabla U(\bar{\boldsymbol{x}}) = \lambda p. \tag{8.7}$$

If we introduce further restrictions on preferences then we obtain some simple first-order conditions. Assume that the consumer preferences are von Neumann–Morgenstern and additively separable over time. That is, the consumer's problem is:

$$\left[\begin{array}{l} \text{Max} \sum_{t=0}^{T} \sum_{e \in E_t} \delta^t u(x(e_t))\pi(e_t) \\ \\ s.t. \sum_{t} \sum_{E_t} p(e_t)x(e_t) = \sum_{t} \sum_{E_t} p(e_t)\bar{x}(e_t) \equiv W_0. \end{array}\right. \tag{8.8}$$

It is important to realize that the probabilities π can be manipulated as conditional probabilities (for more on this see Huang and Litzenberger, 1988: ch. 7).

Now consider the first-order conditions (8.7) when utility is of the form (8.8):

$$\delta^t u'(\bar{x}(e_t))\pi(e_t) = \lambda p(e_t).$$

Of course this is just a special case of (8.7), where prices $\{p(e_t)\}$ will depend upon

$$\{\pi(e_t)\},\ \{\bar{x}(e_t)\}$$

and the specification of the subutility function $u()$. By imposing more structure on $u()$, the probabilities, and endowments, it is possible to obtain closed-form solutions for prices. For example, by assuming that $u(x) = \ln x$ and particular specifications of the probability density it is possible to obtain simple formulae for prices (see Rubinstein, 1976).

As an aside, we should observe that many authors treat the consumer problem via dynamic programming techniques. This is a clumsy way of tackling this problem as it disguises the elementary nature of the consumer's problem.

STOCHASTIC INTEREST RATES

Returning to our general formulation, we will construct a series of interest rates from the Arrow–Debreu prices $\{p(e_t)\}$. Recall the way in which riskless short- and long-term rates were derived in the riskless economy. This derivation did not rely on the simple nature of the economy, but were merely definitions defined on prices.

In the same way we will define contingent or stochastic interest rates. Given an event e_t, consider an immediate successor event e_{t+1}. Define the set of successor events to e_t to be $S(t+1 \mid e_t)$, so that $e_{t+1} \in S(t+1 \mid e_t)$. Define the contingent short rate of return as

$$\frac{p(e_{t+1})}{p(e_t)} = [1 + r(e_{t+1} \mid e_t)]^{-1}.$$

Notice that this rate is *not* riskless in the sense that it represents the rate of return at e_t for an asset that pays one unit if and only if $e_{t+1} \in S(t+1 \mid e_t)$ occurs. To obtain a riskless interest rate contingent on e_t, we define

$$p(t+1 \mid e_t) \equiv \sum_{S(t+1 \mid e_t)} p(e_{t+1}),$$

and

$$\frac{p(t+1 \mid e_t)}{p(e_t)} \equiv (1 + r(t+1 \mid e_t))^{-1}.$$

In this definition $r(t+1 \mid e_t)$ is a conditional short-term interest rate. As we move through the tree it will change in a 'predictable' fashion, i.e. given e_t, then we will know the short rate. But prior to e_t the short rate will depend upon which future node eventuates.

In the same way, contingent long rates can be defined. Given e_t, consider a bond that pays off a unit of the commodity in successor events $S(t+\tau \mid e_t)$. Define

$$p(t+\tau \mid e_t) \equiv \sum_{e_{t+\tau} \in S(t+\tau \mid e_t)} p(e_{t+\tau}).$$

Then the contingent long rate for $t + \tau$, given e_t will be defined by:

$$\frac{p(t+\tau \mid e_t)}{p(e_t)} \equiv [1 + r(t+\tau \mid e_t)]^{-\tau}.$$

PRICE NORMALIZATION

Given the Arrow–Debreu prices, we can generalize our martingale pricing idea, by appropriate normalization rules. To begin, consider an event e_t with $t < T$, with immediate successor events $S(t + 1 \mid e_t)$. Now recall

$$[1 + r(t+1 \mid e_t]^{-1} \equiv \sum_{S(t+1 \mid e_t)} \frac{p(e_{t+1})}{p(e_t)}$$

defines the short rate of interest between e_t and $t + 1$.

Now define

$$q(e_{t+1} \mid e_t) \equiv \left[\frac{p(e_{t+1})}{p(e_t)}\right][1 + r(t+1 \mid e_t)] \quad \text{for} \quad e_{t+1} \in S(t+1 \mid e_t).$$

If $p(e_{t+1})$, $p(e_t)$ are strictly positive then the derived $q()$ is well defined and strictly positive. Also, by construction

$$\sum_{S(t+1 \mid e_t)} q(e_{t+1} \mid e_t) \equiv 1,$$

so that $q()$ has all the properties of a conditional probability measure.

Notice that we have met a special case of this construction before when we discussed the two-date martingale pricing methods with complete markets. We observed that, in general, there did not have to be any simple relation between the $q()$ prices and true probabilities over the states, i.e. the true stochastic process. Of course, that observation applies to our more general multidate construction.

Our derivation of $q()$ was defined recursively over successive dates; but it is easy to extend the argument to non-successive dates. Consider e_t and a date $t + \tau$, $\tau \geqslant 1$. Recall $S(t + \tau \mid e_t)$ as all those successor events at $t + \tau$ that can be reached from e_t; and

$$[1 + r(t + \tau \mid e_t)]^{-\tau} \equiv \sum_{S(t+\tau \mid e_t)} \frac{p(e_{t+\tau})}{p(e_t)};$$

then
$$q(e_{t+\tau} \mid e_t) \equiv \left[\frac{p(e_{t+\tau})}{p(e_t)}\right][1 + r(t + \tau) \mid e_t)]^{\tau}.$$

Clearly, the construction of $q()$ follows all the rules of conditional probability, although $q()$ may not match the underlying probabilities.

Having defined short- and long-term interest rates, and derived martingale prices from Arrow–Debreu prices, we close this chapter by discussing two special economies that provide closed-form solutions for interest rates.

A REPRESENTATIVE AGENT ECONOMY

Earlier in this chapter we discussed a single (representative) consumer economy, where the Arrow–Debreu prices were obtained from the gradient of the utility function at the endowment point. By restricting preferences and the endowment, i.e. the stochastic process describing the endowment, it is possible to obtain closed-form formulae for the interest rates and the q's. Turnbull and Milne (1991) assume the HARA class of utility, and that the endowment growth follows a Gaussian autoregressive process. Using this model they are able to obtain the Arrow–Debreu prices, interest rates, and q's in terms of parameters of the stochastic process. Of course, if the preferences are not differentiable, then the Arrow–Debreu prices, interest rates, and q's will be non-unique. Epstein and Wang (1992) provide a multiperiod example of such a model where the representative consumer has non-expected utility.

PRICES AND PRODUCTION

The representative agent model of asset pricing has been used widely in the literature. But the alternative route of pricing from the production side has seldom been used. Here we will sketch how such a pricing argument can be constructed.

Consider an economy where the firm (or firms) has constant returns to scale technology that satisfies the non-substitution theorem (see Varian (1992), ch. 18). At any event e_t assume that there are coefficients $\alpha(e_{t+1} | e_t)$ of production that give the productivity of a unit of the commodity at e_t, in producing the commodity at e_{t+1}. In equilibrium, firms will earn zero profits and the Arrow–Debreu prices will be determined by the production coefficients. From the definition of the interest rates and the q's, one obtains a pricing and interest rate structure independent of the consumption decisions of consumers. By specifying the evolution of the $\alpha()$'s, one can determine the stochastic process of interest rates and q's.

CONCLUSION

Having introduced the multiperiod Arrow–Debreu economy and normalization schemas for deriving interest rates and martingale prices, we turn in the next chapter to a more complicated asset structure in a complete market economy.

9

General Asset-Pricing in Complete Markets

To introduce more complex assets with multiple pay-offs, we require a construction that introduces asset markets explicitly. At the same time, the construction should be relatively simple to reveal the basics of the general argument.

For expositional ease, consider a three-date world with an event tree that describes a binomial process (Figure 9.1). Notice that there are seven nodes. It will become clear that our argument is quite general and can be extended to multinomial and multidate information trees.

To keep the argument simple, consider an exchange economy where consumers can trade in Arrow–Debreu assets at $t = 0$. Thus a consumer's problem is:

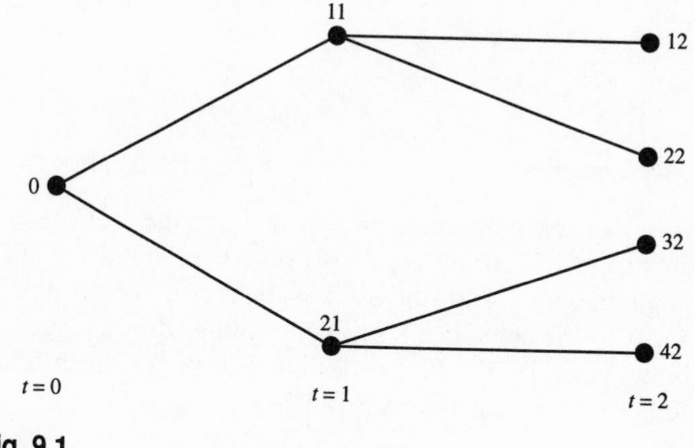

Fig. 9.1

$$\text{Max } U_i(\boldsymbol{x}_i)$$

$$s.t. \quad x_i(0) = \bar{x}_i(0) - \sum_{e_t} p(e_t)a_i(e_t) \tag{9.1}$$

$$x_i(e_t) = \bar{x}_i(e_t) + a_i(e_t), \forall e_t.$$

Problem (9.1) can be written in a more compact form, using vector and matrix notation:

$$\text{Max } U_i(\boldsymbol{x}_i), \tag{9.2}$$

$$s.t. \ \boldsymbol{x}_i = \bar{\boldsymbol{x}}_i + \boldsymbol{R}\boldsymbol{a}_i,$$

where

$$a_i^T = [a_i(11), \ldots, a_i(42)]$$

and R is a matrix (7×6 in our example), where the columns represent the positive or negative pay-offs across events, and the columns represent the different assets (Table 9.1).

TABLE 9.1

		Asset					
		11	21	12	22	32	42
	0	− p(11)	− p(21)	− p(12)	− p(22)	− p(32)	− p(42)
	11	1	0	0	0	0	0
Pay-off	21	0	1	0	0	0	0
over	12	0	0	1	0	0	0
events	22	0	0	0	1	0	0
	32	0	0	0	0	1	0
	42	0	0	0	0	0	1

It is an easy exercise to show that the consumer's sequence of linked budget constraints can be collapsed to a single budget constraint, so that the consumer's problem reduces to the consumer's problem discussed in Chapter 8.

Now, consider the first-order conditions for an interior solution to the consumer's problem:

$$\boldsymbol{\nabla U}_i\boldsymbol{R} = \boldsymbol{0}. \tag{9.3}$$

By the construction of R, ∇U_i will have a unique solution in (9.3). Denote $\nabla U_i = p$, which is the vector of Arrow–Debreu prices. It follows immediately that because asset markets are complete, the economy has an equilibrium which satisfies the first fundamental theorem of welfare economics. That is, (9.3) simply says that all consumers equate their marginal rates of substitution—a necessary condition for a Pareto optimum.

ADDITIONAL ASSETS

We can introduce more complex securities, by adding them to our base Arrow–Debreu asset economy. As an example, consider an asset k' which is traded for the first time at event 11 with a price $-p_{k'}(11)$, and has pay-off at events 12 and 22 of $R_{k'}(12)$ and $R_{k'}(22)$ respectively (Table 9.2). This asset k' has a pay-off vector

TABLE 9.2

	k'
0	0
11	$-p_{k'}(11)$
21	0
12	$R_{k'}(12)$
22	$R_{k'}(22)$
32	0
42	0

Enlarging the R matrix to include asset k' we can write down the first-order conditions for the consumer as in (9.3). It follows immediately that for asset k' we have

$$\boldsymbol{p}^T \boldsymbol{R}_{k'} = 0;$$

or, expanding the equation:

$$p(11)p_{k'}(11) = p(12)R_{k'}(12) + p(22)R_{k'}(22);$$

or

$$p_{k'}(11) = \frac{p(12)}{p(11)} R_{k'}(12) + \frac{p(22)}{p(11)} R_{k'}(22).$$

Recalling our construction of the discounted Arrow–Debreu $q()$ from the previous chapter, we have:

$$p_{k'} = \frac{1}{(1 + r(2 \mid 11))} [q(12 \mid 11)R_{k'}(12) + q(22 \mid 11)R_{k'}(22)].$$

This particular pricing formula is a generalization of our binomial pricing formula from Chapters 4 and 5. Later in this chapter, we will show how such analysis can be undertaken recursively to generate the multiperiod binomial option-pricing formula.

We can generalize our model to allow for additional assets with complex pay-offs by the simple expedient of adding asset return vectors to the R matrix and adding asset trades to the asset vector $\boldsymbol{a}_i$. Thus a competitive equilibrium in our asset economy can be defined as follows:

DEFINITION 9.1. *A competitive equilibrium in a complete asset-exchange economy is price-returns matrix R, consumption plans*

$$[\boldsymbol{x}_i^*, i \in I],$$

and an asset allocation

$$[\boldsymbol{a}_i^*, i = 1, \ldots, I]$$

such that:

(i) $\boldsymbol{a}_i^*$ *solves* $\begin{cases} \text{Max } U_i(\boldsymbol{x}_i) \\ s.t.\ \boldsymbol{x}_i = \bar{\boldsymbol{x}}_i + R\boldsymbol{a}_i; \end{cases}$

(ii) $\sum_i \boldsymbol{a}_i^* = \boldsymbol{0}.$

Given a competitive equilibrium, we can prove an exchange version of our Modigliani–Miller theorem.

THEOREM 9.1. *Given a competitive equilibrium for the asset-exchange economy (Definition 9.1), then if the column rank of R is less than the number of columns (i.e. there are dependent asset returns), then there is a linear manifold of equilibrium asset allocations, and any dependent assets K can be priced by*

$$\boldsymbol{p}^T \boldsymbol{R}_k = 0,$$

where **P** *is the vector of Arrow–Debreu prices.*

Proof. From the definition of the equilibrium economy and the rank condition on R, then clearly there are non-unique equilibrium asset allocations (a linear manifold) solving

$$\boldsymbol{x}_i^* = \bar{\boldsymbol{x}}_i + \boldsymbol{R}\boldsymbol{a}_i^* \quad \text{and} \quad \sum_i \boldsymbol{a}_i^* = 0 \text{ for all } [\boldsymbol{a}_i^*].$$

From the first-order conditions for any consumer (9.3) we have $\boldsymbol{p}^T \boldsymbol{R}_k = 0$.

ASSET ECONOMIES WITH FIRMS

This theorem can be extended to allow for firms and production. In an obvious fashion, consider firms to have the problem:

$$\begin{aligned} &\text{Max } \boldsymbol{p}^T \boldsymbol{x}_j \\ &s.t. \ (i) \ \ \boldsymbol{x}_j = \boldsymbol{y}_j + \boldsymbol{R}\boldsymbol{a}_j \\ &\quad\ \ (ii) \ \ \boldsymbol{y}_j \in Y_j. \end{aligned} \tag{9.4}$$

In words, the firm maximizes its net present value given its constraints on production and its asset portfolio. Notice that because in equilibrium $\boldsymbol{p}^T R = 0$, problem (9.4) collapses to the standard Arrow–Debreu problem:

$$\begin{aligned} &\text{Max } \boldsymbol{p}^T \boldsymbol{y}_j \\ &s.t. \ \boldsymbol{y}_j \in Y_j. \end{aligned}$$

Given the firm's problem, we can generalize our Definition 9.1 to a production economy.

DEFINITION 9.2. *A competitive equilibrium in a complete asset economy with production, is a price matrix R, an asset allocation*

$$(\boldsymbol{a}_i^*, i \in I)(\boldsymbol{a}_j^*, j \in J),$$

and consumption and production vectors

$$(\boldsymbol{x}_i^*, i \in I)(\boldsymbol{y}_j^*, j \in J)$$

such that:

(i) $(\boldsymbol{x}_i^*, \boldsymbol{a}_i^*)$ *solves the consumer problem;*

(ii) $(\boldsymbol{y}_j^*, \boldsymbol{a}_j^*)$ *solves the firm problem;*

(iii) $\sum_i \boldsymbol{a}_i^* = \sum_j \boldsymbol{a}_j^*$;

(iv) $\sum_i \boldsymbol{x}_i^* = \sum_i \bar{\boldsymbol{x}}_i + \sum_j \boldsymbol{y}_j^*$.

As an elementary extension of Theorem 9.1, we obtain the full Modigliani–Miller theorem:

THEOREM 9.2 (Modigliani–Miller). *Given a competitive equilibrium for the asset economy (Definition 9.2), then if the column rank of R is less than the number of columns (i.e. there are dependent asset returns), then there is a linear manifold of equilibrium asset allocations, and any dependent assets k can be priced by*

$$\boldsymbol{p}^T \boldsymbol{R}_k = 0,$$

where $\boldsymbol{p}$ *is the Arrow–Debreu price vector.*

MULTIPERIOD HEDGING STRATEGIES AND ARBITRAGE PRICING

There are two important aspects to Theorem 9.2. The first involves the construction of arbitrage-free portfolios that perfectly hedge the risks of an asset or cash flow. In a two-date model, this is a relatively simple procedure, but for multiple dates we may require complicated contingent portfolio strategies to undertake the hedge. The second aspect of Theorem 9.2 is the deduction of prices from the hedging procedure.

To illustrate these arguments consider the event tree in Figure 9.1. Let the events be described by uncertainty about the return on a share. At each node (before the nodes at $t = 3$) a share price can go either up 'u', or down 'd'. We can set out the return matrix for the case of shares that follow an up–down process; and a sequence of riskless bonds with a constant rate of interest. For the moment we will ignore the Arrow–Debreu securities as represented in Table 9.1.

TABLE 9.3

		Asset					
		S(0)	S(11)	S(21)	B(0)	B(11)	B(21)
	0	$-p_s$	0	0	-1	0	0
	11	up_s	$-up_s$	0	$(1+r)$	-1	0
Pay-off	21	dp_s	0	$-dp_s$	$(1+r)$	0	-1
over	12	0	u^2p	0	0	$(1+r)$	0
events	22	0	udp_s	0	0	$(1+r)$	0
	32	0	0	dup_s	0	0	$(1+r)$
	42	0	0	d^2p_s	0	0	$(1+r)$

The reader can check that the Arrow–Debreu return matrix (Table 9.1) and the share-bond matrix (Table 9.3), both span the pay-off events. Indeed, we can relate the Arrow–Debreu prices to the given parameters u, d, and r, in a generalization of our discussion in Chapter 4. The easiest way to see this is by applying a backward-recursive pricing argument. Consider the node 11. The conditional Arrow–Debreu price at 11 to buy 1 unit of the commodity at 12 is given by:

$$p(12\,|\,11) = (1+r)^{-1}\left[\frac{(1+r)-d}{u-d}\right] \equiv (1+r)^{-1}q_1.$$

Clearly, the hedge is almost exactly as in our discussion in Chapter 4. (As the reader can check, there is an additional u term.)

By the same hedging argument we deduce

$$p(22\,|\,11) = (1+r)^{-1}\left[\frac{u-(1+r)}{u-d}\right] \equiv (1+r)^{-1}q_2.$$

Now consider the event node 21. By the same argument we deduce

$$p(32\,|\,21) = (1+r)^{-1}\left[\frac{(1+r)-d}{u-d}\right] \equiv (1+r)^{-1}q_1,$$

$$p(42\,|\,21) = (1+r)^{-1}\left[\frac{u-(1+r)}{u-d}\right] \equiv (1+r)^{-1}q_2.$$

Having analysed the contingent Arrow–Debreu prices at 11 and 21, we can retreat to the initial node 0. By the same argument we obtain:

$$p(11\,|\,0) = (1+r)^{-1}q_1,$$

$$p(21\,|\,0) = (1+r)^{-1}q_2.$$

Finally, we can chain these arguments together by the observation that a dynamic portfolio of the $(11\,|\,10)$ and $(12\,|\,11)$ securities will provide the same unit pay-off as the original Arrow–Debreu security (12) in Table 9.1. Thus by Theorem 9.1 or 9.2 we deduce that

$$p(12) = (\,(1+r)^{-1}q_1)^2 = (1+r)^{-2}q_1^2.$$

Similarly, we deduce that

$$p(22) = (1+r)^{-2}q_1q_2,$$

$$p(32) = (1+r)^{-2}q_2q_1,$$

$$p(42) = (1+r)^{-2}q_2^2.$$

Because $q_1 + q_2 = 1$, it is easy to see that the Arrow–Debreu prices have the same properties as a binomial stochastic process. The symmetry of the process, and the description of events by the stock price imply that the events are defined independently of the order in which the 'ups' and 'downs' occur. (This is called path independence.) Therefore, we have $p(22) = p(32)$.

It is not hard to show (see Cox, Ross, and Rubinstein, 1979; or Huang and Litzenberger, 1988: ch. 8) that our three-date model can be extended to many periods, $t = 0, \ldots, T$. Furthermore, the simple binomial argument extends so that the event of n 'ups' and $T - n$ 'downs'

(i.e. the share price is $p_s u^n d^{T-n}$)

has an Arrow–Debreu price of

$$(1 + r)^{-T} \frac{T!}{n!(T - n)!} q^n (1 - q)^{T-n},$$

where $q \equiv q_1$ and $(1 - q) \equiv q_2$.

OPTION PRICING

So far we have considered Arrow–Debreu securities and shares and bonds. But our general framework allows us to price any pay-off stream. Recall the call option introduced in Chapter 4. We can extend that simple two-date analysis to many dates. From the general definition of a call option, the return to a call option at maturity date T, with exercise price K, in final state $u^n d^{T-n}$ is:

$$R_c(u^n d^{T-n}) \equiv \text{Max}\,[0, p_s u^n d^{T-n} - K].$$

From Theorem 9.1 or 9.2 we know that the call option can be priced by arbitrage and its return replicated by a dynamic hedge of the share and bond. Thus the price of a call at $t = 0$ is:

$$p_c(0) = (1+r)^{-T} E_q(\tilde{R}_c)$$
$$= (1+r)^{-T} \sum_{n=0}^{T} \frac{T!}{n!(T-n)!} q^n (1-q)^{T-n} R_c(u^n d^{T-n}).$$

Now it is not difficult to show (see Cox, Ross, and Rubinstein, 1979; or Huang and Litzenberger, 1988: ch. 8) that this formula can be rewritten as:

$$p_c(0) = p_s \Phi(j; T, q') - K(1+r)^{-T} \Phi(j; T, q), \qquad (9.5)$$

where

(1) j is the minimum positive integer such that

$$j \geqslant \ln\left[\frac{K}{p_s d^T}\right]\left[\ln \frac{u}{d}\right]^{-1};$$

(2) $\Phi(j; T, q) \equiv \sum_{n=j}^{T} \frac{T!}{n!(T-n)!} q^n (1-q)^{T-n};$

(3) $q' \equiv (1+r)^{-1} uq.$

Equation (9.5) is the binomial option-pricing formula derived by Cox, Ross, and Rubinstein (1979).

It is possible to show that as the number of trials per unit time increases the central limit theorem can be invoked to show that (9.5) converges in an appropriate sense to the celebrated Black–Scholes formula (see Cox, Ross, and Rubinstein, 1979).

MULTINOMIAL MODELS

It should be obvious that the binomial option pricing formula can be generalized to a multinomial pricing formula. Madan, Milne, and Shefrin (1989) consider the case where there are exactly n successors for any non-terminal node e_t. By assuming n independent asset returns, one can derive the Arrow–Debreu prices for the tree. Assuming constant interest rates, it is not difficult to construct a multinomial version of the binomial formula (9.5). By taking appropriate limits it is possible to obtain Brownian motion or Poisson jump limits to obtain a generalization of the Cox, Ross, and Rubinstein analysis.

CONCLUSION

Having constructed a complete market economy that is supported by Arrow–Debreu prices, we turn to the case of multiperiod, incomplete asset-markets.

10

Multiperiod Asset-Pricing: Incomplete Asset-Markets

So far, we have discussed a multiperiod economy with complete asset or Arrow–Debreu markets. In this chapter we will introduce a general structure that allows us to characterize incomplete or incomplete asset-markets.

We do this by introducing asset markets that may or may not span the full event space ($\boldsymbol{E} + 1$). Let there be a set $\boldsymbol{K} = \{1, \ldots, K\}$ of assets that can be traded at different events. By representing asset returns as a matrix R of dimension $(E + 1) \times K$, we can represent returns or dividends as positive components, and prices paid as negative components of the matrix. In other words, we can use our asset return matrix R from Chapter 9, even though the asset markets are incomplete.

Consider the tree structure we discussed in Chapter 8, Figure 10.1. Assume that there are only three assets; asset $k = 1$ can be bought at 0 for a price $p_1(0)$ and held until $t = 2$ where it pays $(R_1(12), R_1(22))$ and zero elsewhere. At date $t = 1$ it pays nothing: this can be interpreted as saying that the market for asset 1 is closed at that date, and reopens at $t = 2$. The second asset, $k = 2$, is not traded at 0, but opens for trade at $t = 1$, event 11, where it can be bought for $p_2(11)$. Subsequently it pays returns $(R_2(12), R_2(22))$ at $t = 2$. Finally, asset $k = 3$ can be bought at $t = 0$ for $p_3(0)$ and returns $R_3(11)$ at event e_{11}, and zero elsewhere.

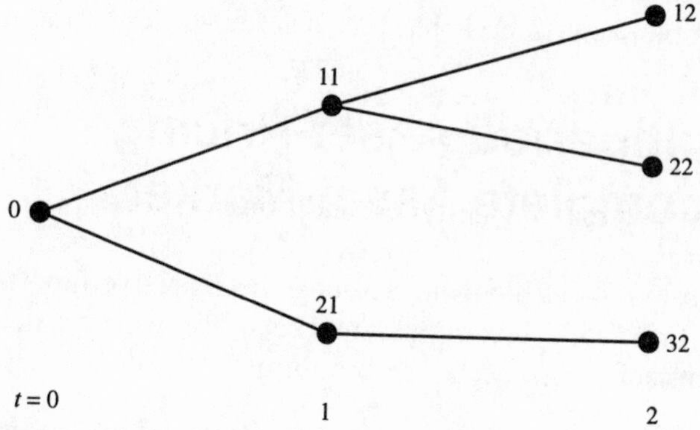

Fig. 10.1

This pay-off matrix R can be represented as set out in Table 10.1.

TABLE 10.1

		k		
		1	2	3
	0	$-p_1(0)$	0	$-p_3(0)$
	11	0	$-p_2(11)$	$R_3(11)$
e_t	21	0	0	0
	12	$R_1(12)$	$R_2(12)$	0
	22	$R_1(22)$	$R_2(22)$	0
	32	0	0	0

Now given this general structure we set out the consumer's problem:

$$\left[\begin{array}{l} \qquad \text{Max } U_i(\boldsymbol{x}_i) \\ s.t.\ \boldsymbol{x}_i = \bar{\boldsymbol{x}}_i + R\boldsymbol{a}_i \\ \boldsymbol{x}_i \in X_i; \quad \boldsymbol{a}_i \in \mathbb{R}^K. \end{array}\right. \tag{10.1}$$

Assuming an interior optimum, $\boldsymbol{x}_i^*$, then the first-order conditions for a maximum are:

$$\nabla U_i R = 0. \tag{10.2}$$

Notice that R has positive and negative elements. For example, asset 2 in Table 10.1 has first-order conditions

$$p_2(11)\frac{\partial U_i}{\partial x_i(11)} = R_2(12)\frac{\partial U_i}{\partial x_i(12)} + R_2(22)\frac{\partial U_i}{\partial x_i(22)}.$$

Later we will interpret these first-order conditions to construct martingale-type conditions on asset-prices and returns.

To avoid problems in defining the objective function of the firm with incomplete markets, we will restrict our discussion to an exchange economy.

DEFINITION 10.1. *In a multiperiod asset-exchange economy, an equilibrium returns matrix R and an allocation* $[(\boldsymbol{x}_i^*, \boldsymbol{a}_i^*)\forall i]$ *satisfies*:

(i) $(\boldsymbol{x}_i^*, \boldsymbol{a}_i^*)$ *satisfies the consumer's problem (10.1):*

(ii) $\sum_i \boldsymbol{a}_i^* = 0$;

(iii) $\sum_i \boldsymbol{x}_i^* = \sum_i \bar{\boldsymbol{x}}_i$.

ARBITRAGE-FREE ASSET RETURNS

The equilibrium asset-returns matrix R excludes arbitrage possibilities, otherwise, we would not have a competitive equilibrium. That is, there is no portfolio $\alpha \in \mathbb{R}^K$ such that $R\alpha \gg 0$. But we can introduce the idea of perfect substitute portfolios, and provide a generalization of the Modigliani–Miller theorem.

Assumption. For some k' there exists

$$\boldsymbol{\alpha} \in \mathbb{R}^{K-1}$$

such that

$$R_{k'} = \sum_{k \neq k'} \alpha_k R_k,$$

where R_k denotes the kth column of R.

Now if you recall our example set out in Table 10.1, and rewrite condition (10.2) for the three assets, we obtain:

$$\text{(Asset 1)}\quad p_1(0)\frac{\partial U_i}{\partial x_i(0)} = R_1(12)\frac{\partial U_i}{\partial x_i(12)} + R_1(22)\frac{\partial U_i}{\partial x_i(22)}$$

$$\text{(Asset 2)}\quad p_2(11)\frac{\partial U_i}{\partial x_i(11)} = R_2(12)\frac{\partial U_i}{\partial x_i(12)} + R_2(22)\frac{\partial U_i}{\partial x_i(22)}$$

$$\text{(Asset 3)}\quad p_3(0)\frac{\partial U_i}{\partial x_i(0)} = R_3(11)\frac{\partial U_i}{\partial x_i(11)}.$$

If the asset returns for 1 and 2 are equal (i.e. $R_1(12) = R_2(12)$, $R_1(22) = R_2(22)$) then manipulating the three conditions, we obtain:

$$p_2(11) = p_1(0)\cdot R_3(11)(p_3(0))^{-1}.$$

Thus, the price of asset 2 at 11 equals the price of asset 1 times the gross rate of return for asset 3. Clearly this is an arbitrage result, in the sense that if this equality did not hold, an arbitrage opportunity would occur. As the reader can check, with the above equality, there are two equivalent portfolios: (*a*) hold one unit of asset 1; (*b*) hold one unit of asset 2 and one unit of asset 3. This implies that our matrix R in Table 10.1 is of rank 2.

Given this example to motivate the idea of arbitrage we can generalize our two-date and multidate Modigliani–Miller theorems:

THEOREM 10.1. *In a multiperiod asset economy, given rank $R < K$ then there is a non-trivial linear manifold of equilibrium asset allocations over which all consumers are indifferent.*

Proof. Given the consumer opportunity sets

$$\boldsymbol{x}_i^* = \bar{\boldsymbol{x}}_i + R\boldsymbol{a}_i,\quad i = 1, \ldots, I;$$

and the asset market-clearing conditions

$$\sum_i \boldsymbol{a}_i^* = 0,$$

we have a set of linear equations in

$$(a_1^*, \ldots, a_I^*).$$

As the reader can check, the null space of these equations is non-trivial.

Clearly this generalizes our Modigliani–Miller and provides a framework for any dynamic arbitrage/pricing result. Notice that over time redundant or derivative asset markets can be opened or closed without altering the contingent consumptions ($\boldsymbol{x}_i^*$) of the consumers, or their welfare.

PARETO OPTIMALITY

We have from our discussions of the Arrow–Debreu economy that given standard assumptions on preferences etc., any Pareto optimal allocation can be supported by a competitive price system. In particular, we have $\nabla \boldsymbol{U}_i = \lambda_i \boldsymbol{p}$ for all $i = 1, \ldots, I$. Now the interesting question is: what are sufficient conditions to ensure Pareto optimal allocations? We will show that a full set of asset markets appropriately defined, or consumer aggregation are sufficient to ensure Pareto optimality. Given these conditions then the asset-pricing condition $\nabla \boldsymbol{U}_i R = 0$, reduces to $\boldsymbol{p} R = 0$.

FULL SPANNING AND PARETO OPTIMALITY

We know from the two-date and multidate problems with spanning of the contingent claims space, that the equilibrium in the asset economy is a full Pareto optimum. For completeness we report what we discovered in Chapter 9.

THEOREM 10.2. *Given an asset market equilibrium with rank* $(R) = E$, *then the equilibrium contingent claim allocation is Pareto optimal.*

Proof. From condition (10.2) $\nabla \boldsymbol{U}_i R = 0$. By the rank conditions, there is only one solution $\boldsymbol{p}$ to $\boldsymbol{p}R = 0$, i.e. $\nabla \boldsymbol{U}_i = \lambda_i \boldsymbol{p}$, for all $i = 1, \ldots, I$ and scalar λ_i. But we know that this is a necessary and sufficient condition for $[(x_i^*)]$ to be Pareto optimal (see Varian, 1992: ch. 17).

From the theorem we have the condition that $\boldsymbol{p}\boldsymbol{R}_k = 0$, for every $k = 1, \ldots, K$. As we will see a little later, this condition can be reinterpreted as martingale pricing, using normalized Arrow–Debreu prices as the probabilities and discount factors.

CONSUMER AGGREGATION AND PARETO OPTIMALITY

An alternative route to Pareto optimality is to consider a representative consumer. The following theorem generalizes our aggregation result in the two-date economy.

THEOREM 10.3. *Given a multiperiod asset economy where each consumer has*:

(i) $U_i(\boldsymbol{x}_i) = \phi_i(\tilde{U}(\boldsymbol{x}_i))$, $\phi_i' > 0$, $\tilde{U}()$ *homothetic*;

(ii) $\bar{\boldsymbol{x}}_i = \theta_i \bar{\boldsymbol{x}}$ *(proportional endowments)*

then there is an equilibrium where:

(*a*) $\boldsymbol{x}_i^* = \theta_i \bar{\boldsymbol{x}}$ for all i;

(*b*) $\boldsymbol{a}_i^* = 0$, for all i;

(*c*) $\nabla \tilde{\boldsymbol{U}}(\bar{\boldsymbol{x}}) = \boldsymbol{p}^*$;

(*d*) the allocation $[(\boldsymbol{x}_i^*)]$ is Pareto optimal.

Proof. From (10.2) we have

$$\phi_i' \ \nabla \tilde{\boldsymbol{U}}(R\boldsymbol{a}_i + \bar{\boldsymbol{x}}_i) R = 0.$$

But $$x_i^* = Ra_i + \bar{x}_i = \theta_i \bar{x},$$

which implies

$$\nabla \tilde{U}(Ra_i + \bar{x}_i) = \nabla \tilde{U}(\theta \bar{x}) = \nabla \tilde{U}(\bar{x}) \equiv p.$$

Clearly the allocation is an equilibrium with the properties (*a*)–(*d*).

We can extend the theorem to the case where the endowments $\bar{x}_i$ can be considered as an endowment of assets, i.e. there exists

$$\bar{a}_i \in \mathbb{R}^K \text{ such that } \bar{x}_i = R\bar{a}_i.$$

Corollary 10.3. Given the hypothesis of the theorem, but

$$U_i(x_i) = \phi_i(\tilde{U}(\bar{x}_i + x_i)), \quad \bar{x}_i = R\bar{a}_i, \text{ for some } \bar{a}_i \in \mathbb{R}^K,$$

then the conclusion of the theorem follows.

INTRODUCING ASSETS

Given that the contingent allocation is Pareto optimal (either because of full spanning or consumer aggregation), consider the introduction of new asset $K+1$ with return vector R_{K+1} and in zero net supply. Intuitively the introduction of this asset will not perturb the allocation, so that in the new equilibrium the asset will be priced such that $pR_{K+1} = 0$, and all consumers will continue to consume (x_i^*).

Notice that the source of this result differs between the spanning formulation and the representative consumer formulations. With full spanning, the $K+1^{\text{th}}$ asset is redundant because its pay-off structure can be replicated by arbitrage. The representative consumer version allows an asset to be introduced which is not spanned by the existing set of assets, but it does not change the endowment of the representative consumer $\bar{\boldsymbol{x}} = \boldsymbol{x}^*$.

PERSONALIZED MARTINGALE PRICING

Just as in the two-date model, we can introduce a normalization trick on the marginal utilities to convert them into personalized 'probabilities'. That is, the normalized marginal utilities will have the same structure as personalized conditional probabilities or Arrow–Debreu prices.

To begin, divide $\nabla \boldsymbol{U}_i$ by the first component

$$U_{i0} \equiv \frac{\partial U_i}{\partial x_i(0)},$$

so that we get:

$$\nabla \tilde{U}_i \equiv \left[\frac{U_{i0}}{U_{i0}}, \ldots, \frac{U_{iE+1}}{U_{i0}} \right],$$

where $U_{ie_t} \equiv \dfrac{\partial U_i}{\partial x_i(e_t)}$. Now define $\sum\limits_{S(t|e_0)} \dfrac{U_{ie_t}}{U_{i0}} \equiv \gamma_i(t|0)$,

and $$\frac{U_{ie_t}}{U_{i0}} \equiv \gamma_i(t|0) \left[\frac{U_{ie_t}}{U_{i0}} (\gamma_i(t|0))^{-1} \right] \equiv \gamma_i(t|0) q_i(e_t|0),$$

where $$q_i(e_t|0) = \left[\frac{U_{ie_t}}{U_{i0}} (\gamma_i(t|0))^{-1} \right].$$

Given strictly increasing utility, then by construction $q_i(e_t|0) > 0$, and

$$\sum_{S(t|0)} q_i(e_t|0) = 1.$$

That is, $\{q_i(e_t|0)\}$ is a personalized Arrow–Debreu 'probability' price over the nodes of the tree at t.

By similar techniques we can construct conditional personalized Arrow–Debreu prices. Consider a date $s < t$ and e_t is a node reached from beginning at e_s. Define

$$\gamma_i(t \mid e_s) \equiv \sum_{S(t \mid e_s)} \left[\frac{U_{ie_t}}{U_{ie_s}} \right],$$

where $s(t \mid e_s)$ is the set of events reached at t, from the event e_s. By monotonicity of preferences and definition,

$$q_i(e_t \mid e_s) \equiv \left[\frac{U_{ie_t}}{U_{ie_s}} (\gamma_i(t \mid e_s))^{-1} \right] > 0, \text{ and } \sum_{S(t \mid e_s)} q_i(e_t \mid e_s) \equiv 1.$$

Clearly, $q_i(e_t \mid e_s)$ has the required conditional 'probability' structure.

Recalling the condition $\nabla \boldsymbol{U}_i \boldsymbol{R}_k = 0$, then it can be written as

$$R_k(e_s) + \sum_{t > s} \gamma_i(t \mid e_s) \sum_{S(t \mid e_s)} R_k(e_t) q_i(e_t \mid e_s) = 0, \qquad (10.3)$$

where e_s is the first time/event that the asset is traded.

Notice that if there is full spanning or consumer aggregation,

$$\gamma_i(t \mid e_s) = \gamma(t \mid e_s),\ q_i(e_t \mid e_s) = q(e_t \mid e_s) \text{ for all } i.$$

That is, the personalized element disappears from the Arrow–Debreu prices, and we obtain the Arrow–Debreu martingale prices of Chapter 9.

Using our general construction, we will sketch a series of basic models that exploit arbitrage or aggregation to price assets. The first two examples assume that interest rates are non-stochastic; the second two allow for stochastic interest rates.

1. Constant Interest Rates and Arbitrage

The simplest example of this idea is the formulation of Cox, Ross, and Rubinstein (1979). In Chapter 9 we outlined this binomial option-pricing model in the context of a complete market with a binomial event tree. But we can obtain the results by embedding the same argument in an incomplete market structure, where the share prices are insensitive to many of the events observed. For example, consider the share at each node to have a pay-off structure, at successive nodes, as follows:

		state	
	1	$p_s u$	
	2	$p_s u$	Up states
	⋮	$p_s u$	
state	s'		
	$s'+1$	$p_s d$	Down
	⋮	⋮	states
	S	$p_s d$	

Technically, we say that the share price is measurable with respect to the coarse information $\{u, d\}$ rather than the finer information $\{1, \ldots, S\}$. Thus the binomial-option pricing technology can be used even though the background uncertainty, and other asset pay-offs, are more detailed than the coarse $\{u, d\}$ information.

Of course this type of argument can be generalized to multinomial spanning arguments, where there is a basic set of assets that span a linear subspace of asset returns. Any new asset in that span can be priced by arbitrage. This is just an application of the Modigliani–Miller Theorem 10.1.

2. Constant Interest Rates and the Representative Consumer

In Chapter 6 we discussed a series of models with a representative consumer in a two-date incomplete market setting. In the original papers, the models were multidate so that one can obtain multidate versions of asset pricing as a natural extension of the two-date model.

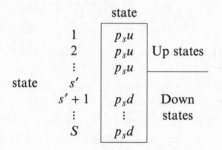

3. Stochastic Interest Rates and Aggregation

Theorem 10.3 and the associated asset-pricing equation (10.3) can be exploited to obtain a general asset-pricing equation with stochastic interest rates:

$$p_K(e_s) = \sum_{t>s} (1 + r(t \mid e_s))^{-\tau} \sum_{S(t \mid e_s)} R_K(e_t) q(e_t \mid e_s). \qquad (10.4)$$

Notice that by aggregation, the Arrow–Debreu prices $q()$ are independent of i, and deducible in principle from the representative consumer's marginal rate of substitution. Because we have assumed stochastic interest rates, and (implicitly) a full set of contingent long bonds, the personalized intertemporal marginal rates of substitution $\gamma_i(t \mid e_s) = (1 + r(t \mid e_s))^{-\tau}$, for all consumers.

In general (10.4) can be applied to a wide variety of homothetic preferences, but the easiest case to consider is the HARA class of von Neumann–Morganstern utility. By choosing an appropriate member of the HARA class and a stochastic process generating the aggregate endowment Turnbull–Milne (1991) were able to produce an Arrow–Debreu measure $q()$ that is sufficiently tractable to generate closed-form solutions for a range of asset prices. For example, they provided closed-form pricing formulae for options on long-term bonds and 'exotic' securities.

4. Stochastic Interest Rates and Arbitrage

We know from Theorem 10.2 that we can deduce the pricing condition (10.4). The two important issues lying behind this pricing relationship are: (i) the derivation of the portfolio that replicates the return stream of asset K; and (ii) the derivation of $q()$ to price the asset. Heath, Jarrow, and Morton (1992) obtained closed-form pricing formulae almost identical to those derived by Turnbull and Milne (1991) by using a continuous time diffusion model. (This simultaneous development of these pricing equations parallel the work of Rubinstein (1976) in obtaining the Black–Scholes option-pricing model from consumer aggregation.)

DISCRETE NUMERICAL METHODS

We have argued that it is possible to obtain closed-form equations for asset valuation from our general finite-time-event tree model by appropriate modifications and simplifications. But it has become apparent that closed forms are the exception rather than the rule, and that many pricing problems defy closed-form solution concepts. This is where the discrete model is useful as a procedure that can be programmed on a computer. Much of the most recent work on asset-pricing on Wall Street uses discrete tree methods to simulate arbitrage strategies, and compute Arrow–Debreu asset prices.

FACTOR PRICING AND DIVERSIFICATION IN A MULTIPERIOD ASSET ECONOMY

In the last three chapters we have discussed arbitrage and representative agent models to obtain general pricing formulae, but we have not discussed factor pricing and diversification. This modification is straightforward in that we can adapt our general APT discussion from Chapter 7 by the simple trick of redoing the analysis conditional on event node e_t. That is, we can obtain conditional APT results at each event node. This methodology has been used widely to analyse stochastic interest-rate models, derivative pricing, and representative consumer models where prices are based upon dynamic factors. For example, the models of Heath, Jarrow, and Morton (1992) and

Turnbull and Milne (1991) exploit this factor interpretation in discussing stochastic interest rates and derivatives based upon bond prices. (For a general survey and synthesis of these ideas, see Milne and Turnbull, 1994.)

INTRODUCING THE FIRM INTO INCOMPLETE ASSET-MARKETS

So far we have avoided introducing firms into the incomplete market setting. With incomplete markets, profit is no longer well defined and the objective function of the firm is problematic. Nevertheless, one might argue that the firm has an objective function that we can encapsulate via a utility function $U_j(\boldsymbol{x}_j)$ over the net (cash) flow $\boldsymbol{x}_j \in \mathbb{R}^{E+1}$. The net cash flow is a residual from the production decisions and asset trades of the firm. As a natural extension of the model of complete markets, in Chapter 9, we obtain:

$$\text{Max } U_j(\boldsymbol{x}_j)$$

$$s.t.\ (i)\ \ \boldsymbol{x}_j = \boldsymbol{y}_j + \mathbb{R}\boldsymbol{a}_j;$$

$$(ii)\ \ \boldsymbol{y}_j \in Y_j.$$

If the firm's preferences are neoclassical then it is easy to extend our analysis in this chapter to incorporate arbitrage arguments emanating from firms. Of course, in the special case of a representative-consumer economy, $U_j()$ should be interpreted as $\boldsymbol{p} \cdot \boldsymbol{x}_j$, the present value of the firm where the Arrow–Debreu prices are derived as supporting prices for the optimal allocation.

CONCLUSION

With the multiperiod, incomplete market economy, we have constructed the most general asset economy used in standard finance models. Much of the analysis can be seen as a natural extension and generalization of our two-date models.

Conclusion

In this book we have surveyed the central ideas underlying recent asset-pricing models: arbitrage, consumer aggregation, and portfolio diversification. We have discussed these ideas in a sequence of increasingly sophisticated models, showing how they can be adapted and illustrated with well-known finance models. In addition we have indicated in passing how recent papers can be incorporated into the framework and can be considered special cases of general theorems.

It is possible to extend the basic ideas in a number of directions to incorporate more sophisticated interactions. For example, we have assumed a single commodity, but it is relatively straightforward to allow for many commodities and spot commodity markets. This allows for: (*a*) real production decisions that incorporate labour and physical capital goods in the firm's planning problem, including discussions of real options; and (*b*) labour, education, and other interpretations of the consumer's intertemporal decision-making.

A second extension introduces money so that the asset-pricing results can be adapted to nominal returns. This allows direct comparisons with macroeconomic models with representative consumers. In addition one can analyse asset returns using arbitrage arguments with nominal returns and the existence of index bonds. A variation on this model introduces multiple currencies so that by taking a partition over agents (countries) the model can be treated as a framework for analysing international finance and asset-pricing.

In discussing arbitrage asset-pricing we used the idea of a factor decomposition. This vector decomposition can be generalized by introducing a more sophisticated notion of a factor that incorporates an underlying probability measure. The idea is to construct an orthonormal basis such that random returns can be written as a linear combination of the orthonormal basis. This construction provides a direct discrete analogue with continuous-time formulations, and taking appropriate limiting arguments one can obtain the continuous-time models in the literature. (For a detailed discussion see Milne and Turnbull (1994).)

Other variations can be introduced that generalize the model in a more realistic and complex manner. Some of the general results are altered or destroyed, but the basic geometric tools continue to be applicable. Two examples of these variations are: (*a*) the introduction of taxation; and (*b*) the possibility of transaction costs in trading assets. These topics are active research areas, but it is possible at this stage to discern how the general models can be adapted to provide useful and instructive results.

Bibliography

Arrow, K. (1963), 'The Role of Securities in the Optimal Allocation of Risk Bearing', *Review of Economic Studies*, 31: 91–6.

Banz, R., and Miller, M. (1978), 'Prices for State Contingent Claims: Some Estimates and Applications', *Journal of Business*, 51: 621–52.

Bernstein, P. (1992), *Capital Ideas: The Improbable Origins of Modern Wall Street* (New York: Free Press).

Bhattacharya, S., and Constantinides, G. (1989), *Financial Markets and Incomplete Information: Frontiers of Modern Financial Theory*, ii (Totowa, NJ: Rowman & Littlefield).

Black, F. (1972), 'Capital Market Equilibrium with Restricted Borrowing', *Journal of Business*, 45: 444–55.

—— and Scholes, M. (1973), 'The Pricing of Options and Corporate Liabilities', *Journal of Political Economy*, 3: 637–54.

Brennan, M. J. (1979), 'The Pricing of Contingent Claims in Discrete Time Models', *Journal of Finance*, 34 (March): 53–68.

—— and Kraus, A. (1976), 'The Geometry of Separation and Myopia', *Journal of Financial and Quantitative Analysis*, 11(2): 171–93.

Cass, D., and Stiglitz, J. (1970), 'The Structure of Investor Preference and Asset Returns, and Separability in Portfolio Allocation: A Contribution to the Pure Theory of Mutual Funds', *Journal of Economic Theory*, 2: 122–60.

Chamberlain, G. (1983), 'Funds, Factors and Diversification in Arbitrage Pricing Models', *Econometrica*, 51: 1305–23.

—— and Rothschild, M. (1983), 'Arbitrage, Factor Structure and Mean Variance Analysis on Large Asset Markets', *Econometrica*, 51: 1281–304.

Chen, N. F., and Ingersoll, J. (1983), 'Exact Pricing in Linear Factor Models with Finitely Many Assets: A Note', *Journal of Finance*, 38: 985–8.

Connor, G. (1984), 'A Unified Beta Pricing Theory', *Journal of Economic Theory*, 34: 13–31.

Cox, J., Ross, S., and Rubinstein, M. (1979), 'Option Pricing: A Simplified Approach', *Journal of Financial Economics*, 7: 229–63.

—— Ingersoll, J., and Ross, S. (1985*a*), 'A Theory of the Term Structure of Interest Rates', *Econometrica*, 53: 385–408.

—— —— —— (1985*b*). 'An Intertemporal General Equilibrium Model of Asset Prices', *Econometrica*, 53: 363–84.

Debreu, G. (1959), *Theory of Value* (New Haven, Conn.: Yale University Press).

Diamond, P. (1967), 'The Role of A Stock Market in a General Equilibrium Model with Technological Uncertainty', *American Economic Review*, 57: 759–76.

Duffie, D., and Huang, C. (1985), 'Implementing Arrow–Debreu Equilibria by Continuous Trading of Few Long-Lived Securities', *Econometrica*, 53: 1337–56.

—— (1986), 'Stochastic Equilibria: Existence, Spanning Number and the "No Expected Financial Gain from Trade" Hypothesis', *Econometrica*, 54(5): 1161–84.

Epstein, L., and Tan Wang (1992), 'Intertemporal Asset Pricing under Knightian Uncertainty' (University of Toronto, Dept. of Economics, WP No. 9211).

—— and Zinn, S. (1989), 'Substitution, Risk Aversion and the Temporal Behavior of Consumption and Asset Returns: A Theoretical Framework', *Econometrica*, 57(4): 937–69.

—— —— (1991), 'Substitution, Risk Aversion and the Temporal Behavior of Consumption and Asset Returns: An Empirical Analysis', *Journal of Political Economy*, 99(2): 261–86.

Fama, E. (1970), 'Efficient Capital Markets: A Review of Theory and Empirical Work', *Journal of Finance*, 25(2): 383–417.

Gilboa, I., and Schmeidler, D. (1989), 'Maxmin Expected Utility with non-Unique Prior', *Journal of Mathematical Economics*, 16: 141–53.

Grossman, S. (1976), 'On the Efficiency of Competitive Stock Markets where Traders Have Diverse Information', *Journal of Finance*, 31: 575–85.

Harrison, J., and Kreps, D. (1979), 'Martingales and Arbitrage in Multiperiod Securities Markets', *Journal of Economic Theory*, 20: 381–408.

—— and Pliska, S. (1981), 'Martingales and Stochastic Integrals in the Theory of Continuous Trading', *Stochastic Processes and Their Applications*, 11: 215–60.

Hart, O. D. (1974), 'On the Existence of Equilibrium in a Securities Model', *Journal of Economic Theory*, 9(3): 293–311.

—— (1975), 'On the Optimality of Equilibrium when the Market Structure is Incomplete', *Journal of Economic Theory*, 22(3): 418–43.

Heath, D., Jarrow, R., and Morton, A. (1992), 'Bond Pricing and the Term Structure of Interest Rates: A New Methodology for Contingent Claims Valuation', *Econometrica*, 60(1): 77–106.

Hirshleifer, J. (1965), 'Investment Decision under Uncertainty: Choice Theoretic Approaches', *Quarterly Journal of Economics*, 79: 509–36.

—— (1966), 'Investment Decision under Uncertainty: Applications of the State-Preference Approach', *Quarterly Journal of Economics*, 80: 252–77.

Huang, C., and Litzenberger, R. (1988), *Foundations for Financial Economics* (North-Holland).

Huberman, G. (1982), 'A Simple Approach to Arbitrage Pricing', *Journal of Economic Theory*, 28: 183–91.

Jarrow, R. (1992), 'Pricing Interest Rate Options', mimeo (Cornell University).

Kelsey, D., and Milne, F. (1992*a*), 'The Existence of Equilibrium and the Objective Function of the Firm' (IER No. 867).

—— —— (1992*b*), 'The Arbitrage Pricing Theorem with Non-Expected Utility Preferences' (IER No. 866; forthcoming *Journal of Economic Theory*).

Lintner, J. (1965), 'The Valuation of Risk Assets and the Selection of Risky Investments in Stock Portfolios and Capital Budgets', *Review of Economic Statistics* (Feb.), 13–37.

Lucas, R. (1978), 'Asset Prices in an Exchange Economy', *Econometrica*, 46: 1429–45.

Madan, D., Milne, F., and Shefrin, H. (1989), 'The Multinomial Option Pricing Model and its Brownian and Poisson Limits', *Review of Financial Studies*, 2(2): 251–65.

—— —— (1991), 'Option Pricing with V. G. Martingale Components', *Mathematical Finance*, 1(4): 39–56.

—— —— (1992), 'Contingent Claims Valued and Hedged by Pricing and Investing in a Basis', forthcoming *Mathematical Finance*.

Markowitz, H. (1959), *Portfolio Selection: Efficient Diversification of Investments* (New York: John Wiley & Sons).

Merton, R. (1973*a*), 'An Intertemporal Capital Asset Pricing Model', *Econometrica*, 41: 867–87.

—— (1973*b*), 'A Theory of Rational Option Pricing', *Bell Journal of Economics and Management Science*, 4(1): 141–83.

Miller, M. H. (1988), 'The Modigliani–Miller Propositions after 30 Years', *Journal of Economic Perspectives*, 2(4): 99–120.

Milne, F. (1974), 'Corporate Investment and Finance Theory in Competitive Equilibrium', *Economic Record*, 50: 511–33.

—— (1975), 'Choice Over Asset Economies: Default Risk and Corporate Leverage', *Journal of Financial Economics*, 2(2): 165–85.

—— (1976), 'Default Risk in a General Equilibrium Asset Economy with Incomplete Markets', *International Economic Review*, 17: 613–26.

—— (1979), 'Consumer Preferences, Linear Demand Functions and Aggregation in Competitive Asset Markets', *Review of Economic Studies*, 46(3): 407–17.

—— (1980), 'Short Selling, Default Risk and the Existence of Equilibrium in a Securities Model', *International Economic Review*, 21(2): 255–67.

—— (1981*a*), 'Induced Preferences and the Theory of the Consumer', *Journal of Economic Theory*, 24(2): 205–17.

—— (1981*b*), 'The Firm's Objective Function as a Collective Choice Problem', *Public Choice*, 37: 473–86.

—— (1988), 'Arbitrage and Diversification in a General Equilibrium Asset Economy', *Econometrica*, 56: 813–40.

—— and Shefrin, H. (1984), 'Clarifying some Misconceptions about Stock-Market Economies', *Quarterly Journal of Economics*, 99(3): 615–27.

—— and Smith, C. (1980) 'Capital Asset Pricing with Proportional Transaction Costs', *Journal of Financial and Quantitative Analysis*, 15(2): 253–65.

—— and Turnbull, S. M. (1994), 'Theoretical Methods for Security Pricing', mimeo (Queen's University, Kingston, Ont.).

Modigliani, F., and Miller, M. (1958), 'The Cost of Capital, Corporate Finance and the Theory of Corporation Finance', *American Economic Review*, 48: 261–97.

Mossin, J. (1966), 'Equilibrium in a Capital Asset Market,' *Econometrica*, 34: 768–83.

Naik, V., and Lee, M. (1990), 'General Equilibrium Pricing of Options on the Market Portfolio with Discontinuous Returns', *Review of Financial Studies*, 3(4): 493–521.

Radner, R. (1972), 'Existence of Equilibrium of Plans, Prices and Price Expectations in a Sequence of Markets', *Econometrica*, 40: 289–303.

Roll, R. (1977), 'A Critique of the Asset Pricing Theory's Tests. Part 1: On Past and Potential Testability of the Theory', *Journal of Financial Economics*, 4: 129–76.

Ross, S. (1976), 'Arbitrage Theory of Capital Asset Pricing', *Journal of Economic Theory*, 13: 341–60.

Rubinstein, M. (1976), 'The Valuation of Uncertain Income Streams and the Pricing of Options', *Bell Journal of Economics*, 7: 407–25.

Samuelson, P. (1965), 'Proof that Properly Anticipated Prices Fluctuate Randomly', *Industrial Management Review*, 6: 41–50.

Sharpe, W. (1964), 'Capital Asset Prices: A Theory of Market Equilibrium under Conditions of Risk', *Journal of Finance*, 19(3): 425–43.

Smith, C. (1976), 'Option Pricing: A Review', *Journal of Financial Economics*, 3(1–2): 3–51.

Stapleton, R., and Subrahmanyam, M. (1984) 'The Valuation of Multivariate Contingent Claims in Discrete Time Models', *Journal of Finance*, 39: 207–28.

Turnbull, S. M., and Milne, F. (1991), 'A Simple Approach to Interest Rate Option Pricing', *Review of Financial Studies*, 4(1): 87–120.

Varian, Hal R. (1992), *Microeconomic Analysis*, 3rd edn. (New York: W. W. Norton)

Werner, J. (1987), 'Arbitrage and the Existence of Competitive Equilibrium', *Econometrica*, 55(6): 1403–18.

INDEX